DRESSAGE
PRIORITY POINTS
Richard Davison

DRESSAGE
PRIORITY POINTS

Richard Davison

Regency House Publishing Ltd.

This book is dedicated to

G.W.D.

Page 1. Richard Davison with Sir Anthony and Lady Bamford's stallion Master JCB (photograph: Susie Lang).

Page 2 Top. Gillian Davison on Lady Bamford's four-year-old No Limit.

Page 2 Bottom. A happy and cheerful Isabel Werth exchanges enthusiastic waves with her fans.

Page 3. Olympic Gold medallist Nicole Uphoff-Becker with Rembrandt in a strong extended canter at the Barcelona Olympic Games.

Above. Isabel Werth rewards Gigolo for a good transition out of the piaffe.

Top Right. Monica Theodorescu and Grunnox Below Right. Isabel Werth and Gigolo.

**Published in 1995
by Regency House Publishing Limited
The Grange, Grange Yard
London SE1 3AG**

ISBN 1 85361 417 3

Designed by Annabel Trodd

Diagrams: Dianne Breeze

ACKNOWLEDGMENTS

When skimming through other writers acknowledgements, I have often wondered why the list appears so long. Is it that they wish to use the opportunity to thank everyone who has helped them on their way through life? Are they taking a leaf out of the televised Oscar awards when, fighting back the tears, the recipients thank the entire cast, every single technician and every friend and relative?

Well, now I know. I will never be so cynical again. The amount of work, commitment and encouragement that my technical advisers and friends have put into motivating and organizing me to write this book has been fantastic.

To name but a few. First, Nicolette and

...abel Trodd from Regency House ...lishing Limited for their original concept, ...Kit Houghton for his striking and expert ...tographs. All of them are absolute profes-...als and perfectionists and have been enjoy-... and stimulating to work with. I must ...nk Michael Seals for always being willing to ...re his computer expertise and rush over at ...oment's notice to sort out the latest crises; ...ristine Ball for spending hours deciphering ...dulcet tones left on the dictaphone, and ...e Kidd for reading the proofs. Susie Lang ...k the photograph of me with Master JCB on ...title page.

Judith and Donald Ingleton-Beer have ...en wonderful in advice and guidance on the ...iting side, as has Penny Goring. They all ...d very busy lives and, although they put on ...ave faces, I can only imagine the groans from ...receiving end of the fax machine as I sent ...em more homework.

My wife Gillian has been, as usual, very ...pportive and helpful in supplying creative ...eas and in proof reading, as have many of ...y students. As it would be unfair to single ...t only a few, it is at this point that I really ...uld get into the Oscar award syndrome and ...t them all, but I will spare you that and ...nply say thank you, you know who you are.

My sincere thanks go to my fellow com-...titors and riders whose photographs we ...ve used to demonstrate their skill in the com-...titors' arena and the fascination, which we ...l share, in training.

I am particularly pleased that Eric Lette, ...hairman of the FEI Dressage Committee ...greed to write the foreword to this book.

CONTENTS

FOREWORD

Accompanying my position as Chairman of the international governing body of dressage are heavy responsibilities and exciting challenges.

First and foremost, it is the primary function of both judges and trainers alike to nurture the principles of classical equitation within the rapidly evolving world of competition dressage. Whilst the basic make-up of the horse has not changed over the centuries, our knowledge and understanding of anatomy, musculature and general horse management and care has increased considerably. The science and possibilities in horse breeding seem limitless, producing an ever-increasing number of talented equine gymnasts for participation in the sport.

To cater for the explosion of interest in dressage throughout the world, the FEI puts much thought and time, in consultation with other organizations such as the International Trainers and Riders Clubs, into designing dressage tests and competitions which allow riders to display their horses' skills, and encourage riders to adhere to a careful, progressive training system. From the tests for young horses until the Grand Prix the emphasis must be on the basic requirements being displayed.

Our sport now attracts much media coverage and the grandstands at major championships now overflow with fans and enthusiasts. Dressage is becoming an exciting spectator sport but, like many other sports, such as ice skating and cricket, it requires an informed commentary in order that spectators understand the intricacies of the rules and the interpretation of the results.

Apart from his successes and achievements as an international rider and trainer, Richard Davison is well known as a good communicator within our sport. I hope you, too, will find his book enjoyable, educative and informative.

ERIC LETTE
CHAIRMAN, FEI DRESSAGE COMMITTEE

ABOVE
Eric Lette and the author in deep discussion at the World Equestrian Games.

LEFT
Monica Theodorescu in full extension on Grunnox

INTRODUCTION

As a professional dressage trainer of long standing, I appreciate the rewards a sound practical training can offer. I also realize that although the trend for dressage pupils to receive professional help is increasing, there will always be a proportion of time when riders must work on their own, at home or at shows.

It is important that every training session, whether under professional guidance or not, is correctly structured in order that students make positive steps forward. No two performances are alike and the suppleness, mood and behaviour of horse and rider will vary from day to day. Why is it that only yesterday, when you were having your lesson, everything seemed to fall into place, yet today, on your own, it is so easy to become disheartened? We must, therefore, be absolutely clear as to the PRIORITY POINTS at each training stage and for each exercise. The establishment of a firm foundation and gradual mastery of the correct 'way of going' are essential. As in any learning process, misunderstandings and uncertainties litter the path to eventual dressage success. There will always be difficult phases to work through. I hope that when you have read through PRIORITY POINTS, you will return to it again and again as a source of useful reference to guide you through any difficult patches you may encounter in the future.

There are many roads to Rome – and as many alternative methods of transport these days. We all have our favourite! The same is true of training horses, although with the formation of national trainer societies and the International Dressage Trainer Club there have emerged generally accepted criteria, to which each individual trainer has contributed his or her own ideas born from their own personal experience.

It is my modest hope that, through this book, I will be able to reinforce the work of my professional colleagues. I hope you will find the summary charts a useful reminder when working through new exercises, or as a source of reference when things aren't going as you would hope. I have included some of my own favourite

exercises that I have found particularly beneficial over the years.

Many dressage riders are lucky enough to have an enthusiastic and dedicated team of supporters. Apart from moral and practical support, riders often rely upon their friends and relatives to act as 'eyes on the ground' and value their observations and comments. However, in order to get the best out of such advice, it is essential that both rider and helper work in the same direction and have the same order of priorities. I hope that dressage observers will find this book as useful as the riders do.

Inexperienced trainee instructors or judges are sometimes more likely to spot faults and mistakes and dwell o them rather more than the good qual ties in a dressage performance. Whi the standard of top international dres sage soars ever higher with result into the 80 per cent region, the perfec performance is always just beyon reach. There are always weak parts i every performance. But how impor tant are these faults and, more to th point, how good are the good parts? hope that this book wi answer these questions, too.

Especially since th advent of the free style t music, or Kur, grandstand at major shows everywher are overflowing. But for th spectators to understand what they are watching also requires an understanding o the significant points. Thi book is designed to help them, too.

In addition to setting ou the PRIORITY POINTS fo both riders and observers, have also tried to touch upor subjects often omitted ir books, but nevertheless fun damental for success in the dressage arena. Warming up management and test riding are just three obvious exam ples.

This book has been written with the intention o making a complex subject easier to understand and to provide a guide to the intricacies of dressage training which will ultimately lead to the world of top class dressage competition.

Richard Davison

CENTRE
Emile Faurie and Virtu demonstrate a classical piaffe.

RIGHT
An earlier spook at the flowers causes no obvious disruption to Rembrandt's balance and expression in the medium trot.

CHAPTER
ONE
The Development of Dressage into an International Sport

The fun and fascination of training dressage horses is certainly not a recent discovery. There is evidence of the Greeks' participation in the Parthenon Frieze and also in the literature of Xenophon, the first great writer on horsemanship. Later, the Romans' interest in horsemanship was diverted to more basic activities, such as chariot racing. The grace and discipline of dressage riding just did not seem to appeal.

The rebirth of dressage coincided with the upsurge of classical art and literature during the Renaissance period when, along with the general revival in cultural interests, dressage was established as an important activity.

The development of the equine gymnast

Young noblemen flocked to the Naples Academy of Federico Grisone, which was established in 1532. Here they discovered different methods of teaching horses to perform intricate and spectacular movements. Soon the fashion had spread from Italy to France, and for the following 300 years the Continental aristocracy immersed themselves in dressage.

In Britain, things were quite different. The lure of the chase in the pursuit of hounds and of the race course winning post commanded everybody's attention.

On the Continent, riding masters and trainers, often retained by the royal courts, evolved a logical and progressive system of training the equine gymnast. They found that encouragement, rather than threatening punishment, was the more effective means of securing a horse's cooperation. Soon the sharp spurs, long whips and atrociously severe bits of early dressage training gave way to more humane equipment.

Highlights of the horseman's calendar were public displays, including the circus,

where rivalry between training methods was keen. It was therefore a logical progression for these demonstrations to develop into dressage competitions as we know them today.

The modern Olympic Games were established in 1896 and at the 1912 Olympic Games, held in Stockholm, equestrian events, together with dressage, were included. Athough the dressage test was really one of basic control, it undoubtedly formed a foundation for future competition. By the 1936 Olympic Games, the standard of performance and the popularity of the sport had started to accelerate. The demanding movements of piaffe and passage were

included and the Grand Prix test, as it is performed today, was already taking shape.

Dressage gets an international organization

An event of great importance for dressage, as for other equestrian events, was the formation of a new international administrative body, the Fédération Équestre Internationale (FEI), in 1921. Its purpose was not only to control the rules and regulations of international equestrian competitions, but to develop equestrian sport, including dressage, on a worldwide basis. The fact that in today's international dressage competitions we see representatives from all over the world – from Japan, New Zealand, Australia, ermuda and a strong team from the United tates, as well as from the longer stablished dressage countries – clearly emonstrates the effectiveness of the work f the FEI.

The FEI at work

efore a horse and rider can enter an international competition, they must first be recomended by their own governing body, nown as their national federation, which in urn, must be affiliated to the FEI. An official assport, containing comprehensive competion details, is issued for each horse.

The FEI must approve every internaional competition. With the horses' welfare lways its top priority, the FEI demands trict standards of facilities and organizaion. Its concern for the horses' welfare xtends further than the competition arena tself, with veterinary examinations and upervision by official stewards constantly n operation in the stabling and warming ıp areas.

It is important that horses have as much est as possible; for this reason, the stables ıre regarded as a high security area, prohibted to members of the public and often even o members of the press.

The night before each international class, ın official draw takes place to determine the order of starting. All riders hope for a late draw and, as in every other competition, nobody wants to start first. In team competitions, the team leader or chef d'équipe, who is not a rider himself, will attend this draw and any other meetings in order to keep his team fully briefed and to put forward the riders' point of view.

The starting order will then be published. It is not unusual at international competitions, in order to fit two or three classes in on one day, for the timetable to start early in the morning, perhaps at 7.00 am, and not finish until late at night, sometimes as late as 11.00 or even midnight.

International judging standards in place

Much effort and hard work goes into the training and upgrading of judges around the world. Although judges come from different countries and will have been trained through their own national training system, they will also have attended official courses

run by the FEI. Each will hold different qualifications according to the standard of their judging experience.

A candidate judge is the first step on the international judges' ladder. The next stage is to become a fully qualified international judge, then an official judge. Official judges are allowed to judge at FEI championship competitions, that is Olympic, World and European championships and major finals.

Conscientious and hard working, judges take their responsibility as custodians of the classical art of dressage extremely seriously and their dedication is second to none. They realize that their job, at the topmost level, is not merely that of appraising equestrian skills but of evaluating the art of equitation itself, for it is important that the sport of dressage remains an art form. With the development of the Kur, or free style test to music, riders have been given a great opportunity to display their artistic skills in their interpretation of the music and development of interesting and elegant choreography.

Judging the competition

Of the five judges in an international competition, two sit on the long sides of the arena, facing each other at the E and B markers, and three on the short side by the C marker (see

ABOVE
Especially since the advent of the free style, international dressage now attracts much media interest.

LEFT
There are five judges placed at different points around the arena. Here the Chief Judge sitting at C returns a competitor's salute. He is accompanied by his secretary, the official course keeper and the computer operator.

diagram, right). The test is divided into a series of movements, each movement being marked out of a maximum of 10.

According to the composition of each test, certain movements are given priority by the inclusion of a co-efficient, in other words a multiplying factor, normally times 2. However, in the free style to music, the compulsory movements may be performed in any order and extra marks are allocated for artistic interpretation, suitability of the music and the degree of difficulty of the composition. The Kur is tremendously popular with audiences around the world and is usually a sell-out event.

The technical tests are introduced in a logical progression up from the easiest of

the Prix St. George on to the more difficult Intermediare I and II, to the Grand Prix, which is used in deciding team competitions, and finally to the highest test for individual champions, the Grand Prix Special and the Kur.

After each competition the riders will receive a copy of the judges' sheets, which contain their comments, criticisms and marks. Often a breakdown is produced of the individual placing of each competitor by each judge. This allows the judges to see how their particular order and marks compare to that of their colleagues. Much constructive discussion takes place between judges and also among judges, riders and their trainers.

Often, members of the public may be confused by the differences in the total marks given by each individual judge; but one must remember that the judges at the side, at E and B, have a completely different viewpoint from those at the short end and their attention is focused on quite different aspects of the performance.

The development of the international dressage horse

The growth in popularity of international dressage has been dynamic. The time when one could identify horse and rider combinations by the riding style and training techniques of their country of origin has now long passed.

In the past, a French rider on an elegant

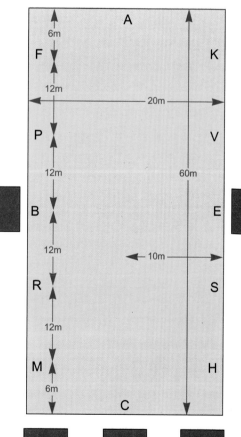

Thoroughbred horse, whilst perhaps lacking the accuracy and precision of a German combination, would gain marks for individual flair and *joie de vivre*. The Russian competitive riders, riding horses of a similar type to the French, would be distinctive for their horses' high head carriage – the result of the influence of an Englishman, James Fillis, who at the turn of the century, moved from France to the Russian cavalry school. The German and the Swedish cavalry schools, who had prolific breeding programmes, required a training system which was designed to develop and supple the rather thicker set and heavier type of horse.

Nowadays, however, the sport has united the world in the development of the dressage horse and influenced breeding programmes. In general, we see a lighter, more athletic type of horse, nearer in looks to the Thoroughbred but with the muscular strength and amenable temperament characteristic of the warmblood.

The competition sport has broken down the barriers which reflected naturalistic style, type of horse and temperament and given us an accepted type or goal for which to aim. As with any other modern sport, competitors, together with owners, grooms and trainers, spend much time together on the international show circuit, which allows not only for a feeling of camaraderie but an interchange of knowledge, advice and horsemanship.

Dressage competition is a test of a combination of qualities, type of horse, temperament of horse, and skill of riding but perhaps, most important of all, the skill of training. As breeding policies around the world have found a common line, so too have training methods. Whilst each horse has an individual temperament, physical strengths and weaknesses, there is a generally accepted and – thanks to the influence of the International Dressage Trainer Club – a general concensus as to the ladder of training.

ABOVE
It isn't only the horse that the top riders must learn to handle. Here, Carol Lavell, a member of the U.S. team, faces a barrage of questions from the press.

BELOW
An example of an FEI Test sheet, reproduced with their permission.

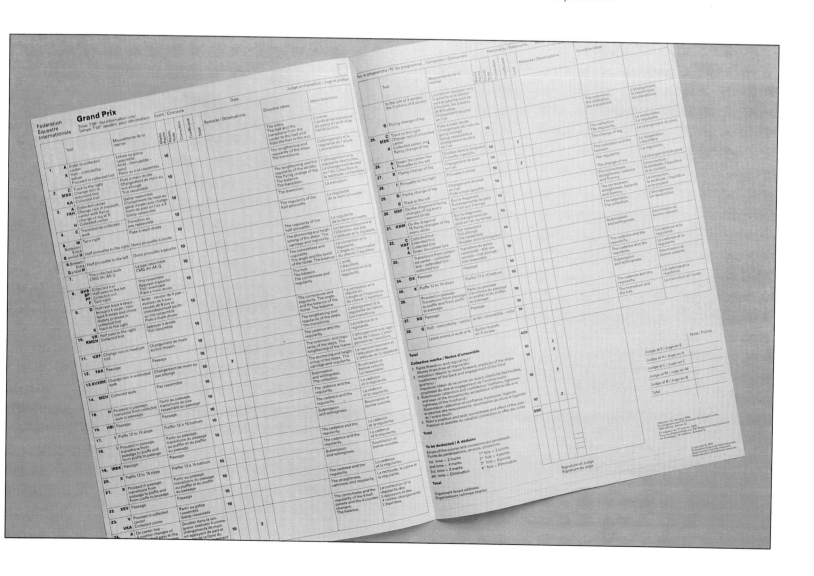

CHAPTER
TWO

Choosing a Dressage Partner

hoosing a partner to live with is difficult enough. Choosing one to both work and live with is extremely difficult! Unfortunately, it is even less easy when it comes to choosing our equine partners.

What are the priorities that you should take into consideration when selecting a horse for the top sport?

- Look for three correct, rhythmical and expressive gaits.
- Supple and loose body muscles.
- Straight and powerful action – the appearance of 'well oiled' joints and free upward-moving shoulder action.
- The ability to develop natural balance, allowing some of the weight of the forehand to be transferred back to the hind legs.
- Add to this, elegant looks with a pretty head and then all you have to do is decide on the colour of your choice and hey presto, off we go!

Wouldn't it be lovely if it was as easy as that. The bad news is that if you wish to own the perfect horse, you will have to draw a picture of one, because the reality is that even if we have assessed our horse thoroughly, there will always be one or two risky areas. And I have not yet even mentioned what is probably the most important factor: the horse's temperament.

Temperament a priority point

It is no good having a super model of a horse if it has not got the right aptitude for learning and a heart big enough to keep trying when the chips are down. There are, perhaps, only a few horses in the world that combine both the physical and mental qualities that I have briefly outlined. These are, of course, real gems and very hard to find.

However, I have a rule of thumb which is that the amateur rider must never

compromise on the horse's temperament. I am not using 'amateur' in the context of ability or standard, more in terms of loving and being dedicated to their sport.

The professional normally has every facility available, including indoor and outdoor schools, turning out paddocks, help on hand, mirrors, videos, horse walkers, gallops and so on. It is generally quite easy for the professional to structure the timetable of the day around the horse's requirements. The professional's life centres wholly on dressage and everything else takes second place.

To the amateur, for whom riding is just one of many aspects of their life, time is a

precious commodity. The one thing you need, when you train animals, is time; not so much when everything is going well, bu especially when you are working through difficult patch. You must allow time fo patient explanation, time to think of new ways of approaching an area of confusion within your horse, time to warm him and cool him down properly.

Training a horse is like educating a child Although fascinating, it is a long-term project and certainly has its ups and downs Horses with difficult characters only serve to slow that process down. Less experienced riders or trainers, working with horse:

which do not have a natural aptitude, may find the training process so slow that it seems to be going nowhere. It is at this point that extreme despair and frustration are likely to set in.

The professional, however, whose job it is to cope with horses of differing characters, must find the know-how and skill to channel the horse's intentions so that they become at one with his own. This is much easier to achieve when the correct facilities are at hand. We all know how difficult it is to encourage a horse to concentrate when we are attempting to school him in the middle of a 20-acre field on top of a windy hill. It is so much easier in an enclosed indoor school.

It is important to realize that, with experience, we can learn to look for the signs that may indicate a difficult temperament. When trying out a horse, in an attempt to discover his likely attitude to training, note his reaction to your leg aids. Does the horse put his ears back, swish his tail and react aggressively to the leg, or does he quietly move forward in an obliging way? Try riding him away from the stables or away from the other horses and see how bravely he copes with this.

Is he a spooky horse? This can be extremely tiresome and distracting for the rider. Likewise, the two extremes of temperament, cold and lazy, or hot and oversensitive can be problematic for the less experienced rider to motivate. Of course, it is not really possible to accurately assess a horse's temperament or attitude under the normal trial conditions in which we have to choose and buy dressage horses. It often takes up to six months to get a real picture.

The entry fee

People do dressage for many reasons. We all realize that 'there are many roads to Rome', but it is important to sit down and accurately work out just what we wish to get out of

dressage. We must then work out how much time, knowledge, skill, and – yes, I'm afraid money – is available.

I always think it is rather like travelling. If you simply wish to get to the best places fast, and you can afford it, why not hop on Concorde and you will be at your destination in an hour or two, totally fresh and ready for action. You will, of course, have seen very little of the world and it can hardly be described as real travel, more like a period spent in a time capsule. There are people who can afford to buy a top Grand Prix horse, thereby short-circuiting the training, making rapid progress, and able to start their dressage career at a high level.

At the other extreme, we have hitch-hiking, a much cheaper form of travel. It is also much more appealing to those who enjoy all the fascinating experiences and personal involvement along the way. However, it takes a great deal longer and, as is the case of so many hitchhikers, they do not always take the direct route. Instead, they zig-zag from one interesting place to another, often becoming distracted from their original destination, perhaps never even getting there, but having a jolly nice time along the way.

The dressage hitchhiker, on grounds of cost, probably has to buy a young, green horse and start from scratch. In other words, some people are more interested and derive more satisfaction from the training aspect, while others are motivated only by participation in sport and competitions. We are all different, thank goodness, and it is a question of making an honest and accurate assessment of our own abilities.

In between these two extremes we have, perhaps, the more normal mode of transport; that of the car travelling along the motorway. Even this, though, can be compared to our training curve, for when you hit a traffic jam on the motorway, the equivalent of hitting stumbling blocks and down points in the training process, do not be tempted to take the first exit off and find the short cut across country lanes.

We have all tried this at some point or other and are still tempted to do it, but how many times does it really work? Very seldom. All it seems to do for me is to add extra time to the journey. So beware of short cuts in your training unless you really know where you are going.

Younger horses, three and four years old, are, of course, cheaper in price. However, they should only be ridden by bold and brave riders who are confident and experienced enough to handle a young horse's freshness and vigour when he squeals and bucks, as any young horse worth his salt will, and to ride forward in a positive and relaxed way.

I would not recommend young horses to people who have limited facilities on the grounds that you need at least an enclosed area, if not an indoor and an outdoor school, in which to back a young horse; one also often needs the help of a lead horse to encourage the horse to go forward on rides throughout the countryside.

Does the horse handle well?

The question of assessing how nice the horse is to handle, in the stable and horse box at a show, is of particular concern to the professional rider's groom as well as to the amateur. The professional rider is unlikely to be as well-acquainted with his horse as the rider who has no extra help on hand to help with grooming and cleaning and that all-important personal contact.

For the professional rider whose groom is an intermediary between himself and his mount, a grumpy horse in the stable is of little concern. For the amateur, it can be more of a problem: if horse and rider have already fallen out, before the training session has even begun, it would hardly be surprising if they got off to a poor start!

Likewise, a horse that is difficult to load on its own can be a great cause of frustration: the professional rider generally has helpers and other horses to encourage maximum safety in this area.

Stallion, mare or gelding?

The fashion for amateur riders to own a stallion goes in waves. Having had, and competed internationally with many stallions myself, I am only too aware of the pros and cons. An alert, shiny-coated, muscle-rippling stallion makes a stunning and eye-catching picture. However, a stallion's concentration can very easily be made to wander and you can suddenly realize that you have only 30 per cent of the horse's attention, especially in the breeding season.

I have also seen some very nasty accidents with inexperienced handlers. A loose stallion galloping around the showground can be extremely dangerous. On the plus side, they can be extremely sensitive and very quick to train but are also, undoubtedly, more mentally complex. The well-muscled neck may look attractive, but in some breeding stallions it becomes so thick and heavy that it does little to help the horse's balance or suppleness.

Having said that, I think there is a great danger of generalizing. We must judge all horses as individuals, and I put forward these guidelines only to enlighten those with no previous experience in handling stallions. People often ask me if I have a preference between mares and geldings. This is, again, where one has to judge the individual. I can give many examples of temperamental geldings and level-headed mares to counteract the fallacy of the hot-headed chestnut mare syndrome.

There are undoubtedly some mares which, when they come in season, have a very difficult time, physically as well as mentally, and when it comes to organizing competitions, this is not easy to plan around. But there have also been some brilliant competition mares and would be a lot more if only people would give them a chance.

One has to be honest about one's own style of riding. If you are an authoritative, motivating type of rider, you may have the dash and expertise to encourage a rather lazy or even ungenerous horse around to your way of thinking. On the other hand, the quieter, more gentle type of rider may well be suited to a slightly hotter, more sensitive type of horse. It is all a question of achieving the right combination between type of rider and type of horse.

It is vital that the horse is the right size for the rider. I don't mean just in terms of height, but in terms of bulk and size of body, which is perhaps even more important.

We have all seen small, short-legged people struggling on heavy-topped, strong warmbloods. It is not impossible for this combination to be a success but it is certainly a great deal more difficult.

The right type and advice

The modern-day dressage horse is definitely of the lighter type, with more Thoroughbred breeding within its pedigree. This allows it to dance through the gymnastic exercises of the Grand Prix test. Horses with very big gaits, with slow-moving hind legs, may have a lovely set rhythm but it can be much more difficult to collect and transfer the weight back on the hind legs. Such horses may not have quick enough reactions and the dexterity to negotiate with success an

ABOVE
A Grand Prix horse should display a natural athleticism and be sharp enough to react quickly to the demands of the test.

RIGHT
A hopeful one for the future. The author inspects a foal sired by his medal-winning stallion Master JCB.

International Grand Prix test: they may, however, be useful small tour Prix St. George or Intermediare I horses.

If you are not very strong, you should beware of buying heavy-topped horses which can become too strong, easily fall on to their forehand and have neck and body muscles which can become very solid and bulky. These muscles should be of the right tone. Imagine a human weight-lifter or nightclub bouncer. Whilst they may be very powerful and strong, it would be inappropriate for them to take part in a sport such as gymnastics, where they are expected to dance through floor exercises or perform delicate backward somersaults on the bar with grace and ease.

It can therefore be seen that there are many factors to take into account when choosing and buying a horse. I would always recommend that you pay your dressage trainer to give a professional assessment as to the suitability of any proposed purchase.

This is, of course, relatively easy if you are buying horses in your own country but gets more complicated and expensive with travelling costs if you are buying abroad. However, any attempt to save on a professional opinion as to a horse's suitability is, I think, as much a false economy as it would be to avoid having a surveyor check your house before you sign the contract.

Buying privately has, of course, many advantages, the most obvious being that the horse can be tried at least two or three times, often in different situations. It is possible to research the horse's record and form through the National Federation and you can send your own vet to examine the horse in his own time.

Going, going, gone!

With breed societies throughout the world producing more and better quality dressage horse young stock, auctions are now increasing. An advantage of auction sales is that they cut down on the amount of travelling you have to do to look at horses as you may be able to see 30 or 40 good-quality horses all in one place.

The established, reputable auctions have thorough vetting and warranty procedures. Trial facilities are generally good and

there is usually much information put forward as to the horses' pedigrees. The breed societies' own auctions, especially in Europe, are an education in their own right.

When it comes to price, people often ask what a particular horse is worth and I have to say that it depends on what it is worth to you. Market forces determine horse prices as they do any other item. If two or more people want the same horse, and they have enough money available, then the price will naturally go up. It is as simple as that.

I have attended many auctions and I am always intrigued as to the degree to which the excitement and spontaneity of the event encourages people to spend their money. Think how often even a professional auctioneer's opinion as to the guide price differs from the one for which the horse, antique, painting or whatever is eventually sold. Many of the world's greatest dressage horses started their career being sold through a breed society auction.

If buying from a country other than your own, you must take into account currency exchange rates, transport and

quarantine costs, if applicable, and the sale and warranty laws under which the horse is being sold. Your veterinary surgeon will give you advice as to the method and procedure for examining the horse for health and soundness.

If you intend to insure your horse, you should consult your insurance company for their vetting requirements before you make your purchase. Some insurance companies will only accept their own veterinary advisers and it would be wise to find this out beforehand.

Transporting your horse from other countries is not really a problem tthese days as the worldwide transportation of horses has become relatively easy in recent years. Transporting horses by air from continent to continent is a regular occurrence and generally causes little stress or after-effect. Horses travelling long distances by road should do so only in well-ventilated and safe transporters and be rested and offered refreshment every four or five hours. Always seek advice from the most reputable transport agent.

CHAPTER
THREE

Management of the Dressage Horse

Newcomers to dressage often worry about the general management of dressage horses. 'How often should I school them? Should I turn them out in the paddock? Is it wrong to jump them? I would like to tell you here how I look after the well-being of my dressage horses.

We school the horses three to four times a week, depending on their age, state of maturity and phase of training. Taking into account the peaks and troughs of the learning curve, it is sometimes better to school a horse four times a week for short periods, if it is going through a particular phase, in order to secure comprehension: while at other times it is better to leave off and only school him two or three times.

There is no fixed rule on this and it can only be a guideline. Like any other form of education, one needs to be flexible and open-minded enough to experiment with whatever suits the individual horse.

Bringing variety to your schooling

We are lucky enough to have two schooling surfaces. One is outdoors and one indoors. The indoor school is open on the sheltered side, which not only allows in sunshine but prevents the horses from feeling claustrophobic. It also means that they become accustomed to dogs running around and to the general hurly burly of life.

It is unwise to limit the training of your horse solely to the indoor school. Enclosed on all four walls, it can come as a very nasty shock when the horse is introduced to the busy showground. We pay great attention to the surface of the school which, in general, I prefer to be not too deep and slightly on the firm side. This is better for the horses' joints and also means that when you go to competitions and have to compete on hard-going surfaces, they won't find them too different.

Surfaces containing a high proportion of rubber can give the rider a very false, yet comfortable feeling. It can make your horse

feel athletic even when he is not. Training every day on surfaces such as these means horses can be rather fussy when faced with the wide variety of competition surfaces.

On days when the horses are not being schooled they go out hacking, at least one day a week. This is not only important for their general fitness and healthy constitution but it also helps with their mental attitude. They need to become accustomed to the sights and sounds of the outside world, and although the young horses always go out in company with the older horses, they must learn to be brave enough to go out on their own.

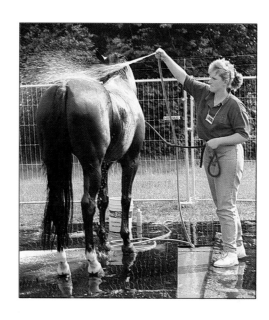

Whilst they are out hacking they are made to walk out in a very purposeful way. There is nothing worse than horses being allowed to slop along lazily when being exercised. Having said that, I do not ask my riders to exercise their horses on the bit, although I don't particularly want their heads stuck up in the air, which can encourage a hollowing in the back. There is a balance to be struck in as much as it is the horses' day off and I like them to be allowed complete freedom of their heads and necks. With at least 95 per cent of their schooling

ensuring that they work in a rounded outline way, there is no problem with correct muscle development.

Alternatively, if appropriate, there is nothing wrong with the inclusion of a bit of schooling whilst out on your hack. From a psychological point of view this can be most advantageous. For example, when you turn for home and the horse is thinking and moving actively forward, it may be quite a good time to revise a particular exercise. Perhaps some leg yielding, moving forwards and sideways, could be tried, or even a bit of piaffe or passage introduced, or, if you are on good going, why not work on the horse's medium trot? However, this has its obvious dangers if you are restricted to busy roads and is therefore only recommended in an 'off-road' situation.

We also believe that basic gymnastic jumping training is good for every horse and especially for the young horses. One needs a good sound knowledge of correct distances and construction of fences. The fences need not be high, but the knowledge of a good jumping technique complements the work on the flat. It does add variety but, like all training exercises, it depends how well it is done.

Other forms of exercise

We also include sessions on the lunge. When the older horses are being lunged, they are made to work actively forwards and in a correct and supple outline. They are not allowed to buck and leap around, as this is often when fit horses strike into themselves or injure their muscles in some way. I also like to vary the placing of the circle, within the arena, and therefore walk my circle, in a controlled manner, up and down the school. This leads to less strain on the horses and more variety to their work.

For approximately five-year-old horses onwards, depending on their maturity, I introduce work 'in-hand'. This is a progressive system of encouraging the horse to take

*It couldn't happen without them. The grooms'
dedication and care are very much appreciated by
horses and riders alike.*

*LEFT
A refreshing shower in the sunshine.*

*BELOW
Like most boys, washing behind the ears is
something Gigolo would rather avoid.*

more weight on the hindquarters and is when he begins to learn about true collection. Ultimately, of course, this work results in the piaffe, but before the piaffe materializes it is a very useful progressive training aid which can benefit the half-trained horse as well as the more advanced. It requires a thorough knowledge and understanding of the aims and objectives, as well as the dangers and pitfalls, and should only be done by a specialist.

Don't forget to turn them out

Our own horses are turned out in paddocks every day for approximately an hour. If this is part of your horse's usual routine I feel it is very beneficial. It allows them to move around and prevents them from getting stiff in a stable. It is very good for them to get their head and necks down and to get some sunshine on their bodies and a bit of grass.

However, especially in summer, one must be careful how much grass they get to ensure that this does not upset the metabolism and cause them to put on too much

weight. We always turn our horses out in their paddocks in boots to prevent injury should a fit horse suddenly become skittish and decide to have a party!

If your horse is not used to going out you must be very careful how you introduce this, especially if the horse is fit, as it is so easy for them to injure themselves. I find that with excitable horses, turning them out calms them down a great deal; sometimes it can be quite useful to leave them out for quite a long while on the day before or even the morning of a competition. Mentally, this can be very useful.

We are also lucky enough to have a horse walker. We use this to ensure that after the horses are worked and washed down they are walked long enough to be really dry before they return to their stables. In an ideal world, with lots of money and plenty of grooms, horse walkers and other mechanical gadgets would not be necessary, but sadly we are not in such a position. We use the walker to give the horses ten minutes' walk exercise during the afternoon. This is particularly valuable for the older advanced horses who benefit from the occasional stroll to stop their muscles from stiffening up.

Day-to-day care

The construction of a stable can vary from the basic to the absolutely luxurious; but the important priorities are that it is large enough for the horse to move around and lie down and roll, without getting cast, and is adequately ventilated with a good air quality and without the problem of draughts. I like to supply my horses with plenty of bedding to avoid injury and good drainage to avoid any stale smells.

Our dressage horses are not shod in any particularly special way; having had the same farrier for very many years, we have developed a good relationship and can discuss any individual requirements. If any of our younger horses are about to compete on grass, we like to supply stud holes in order that we can choose the correct stud for the type of going on which the horse will be competing.

As for feeding, we follow the normal rules which apply to any other horse. Mainly, we feed according to the work done and we also feed according to

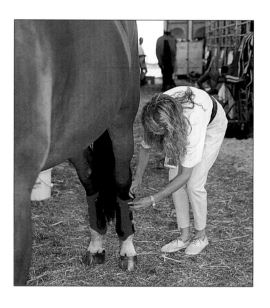

age, physical maturity and temperament. We take into account any days' rest or lay off the horse is about to have. If we are going on a long journey to an international show then naturally we cut the horse's feed down accordingly.

We are very lucky to have expert veterinary advice in that, like my farrier, I have had the same vet for more than 25 years. I believe, though, that if we have any special problems they require an expert in the field. I am fortunate in that the veterinary surgeons who advise me have a great interest in dressage and understand the sport and what it entails. They are more than happy to come and watch the horses working and we work very much as a team.

Tack

Saddlery can be a very expensive item. As with all sports equipment, there is a section of the public who feel that if they spend a great deal of money on equipment, their performance will undoubtedly improve. Sadly, it is not as simple as that and you must still be prepared to put the maximum of time and energy into your training.

There is now a bewildering array of dressage saddles on the market and I always think that choosing a saddle is very much a matter of personal preference.

An important point to consider, when buying this type of saddle, is that it must fit the horse correctly. By this, I mean that the bearing surface which sits on the horse must be as broad as possible so that the pressure is not located in any one small area but distributed over a wide bearing surface. It must be wide enough for the horse and not cause any restriction to his muscular freedom.

From the rider's point of view, the saddle must be the right size and it must be in balance. By this, I mean that if the rider is sitting in the correct position, the saddle must not encourage him to tip forward or backwards. Naturally, it must be laterally equal and balanced – certainly not lower on one side then the other.

One should bear in mind that a young horse changes shape as he matures and his muscles develop. Therefore, saddles need annual attention by an expert to ensure that they are reflocked accordingly.

The dressage fraternity has undoubtedly made tack suppliers very rich and none more so than the bit makers. As time goes by there are ever-increasing numbers of new

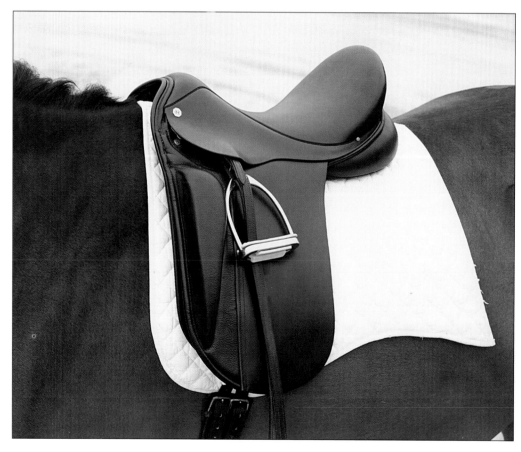

bit designs on the market, all promising to give instantaneous magic results. Sadly, I can honestly say that this has not been my experience.

The priorities for a bit are that it must fit the horse's mouth and not be too wide or too narrow so that it causes pinching on the sides. Additionally, very thick bits can be rather clumsy for narrow-mouthed horses. The point here is that one must consider the structure of the horse's mouth and how the bit lies when the horse is in the outline and working position. I'm afraid I take a very jaundiced view when it comes to bits and stick with the tried and tested principle that it is not what the bit can do for you but rather your training that counts. All my horses' basic work is done in a snaffle of one form or another.

I do believe in using flash nosebands as I think that correctly fitted, they discourage horses from opening their mouths and becoming too strong during difficult phases of training. In an ideal world and if we were all perfect, we wouldn't need such help but I feel that it is only a small artificial aid and one has to be practical.

At international competitions it is compulsory for horses to wear a double bridle. I personally wish this wasn't the case as I consider that some horses undoubtedly find them rather clumsy. However, what must be, must be. We often introduce our horses to double bridles on days when they hack out, or when they are not working particularly hard, until they accept them and become accustomed to them.

The important point when riding with a double bridle is that one should ride 99 per cent on the snaffle rein with the usual elastic contact. The curb rein should have very little weight in it and all the fingers must be closed firmly around the rein to prevent any slipping or maladjustment of the rein contact.

Other helpful aids

As to other gadgets, I prefer not to use them. However, with horses I have to re-train or with very difficult horses, running or draw reins may be useful for a short time. My guidelines regarding their use are that they must only be used by an experienced trainer who is effective in getting the horse forward

and 'in front of the legs'. Secondly, the rider must be capable of riding 99.9 per cent of the time on the normal snaffle rein, only using the running rein momentarily during a half halt.

Just because the horse is wearing running reins does not mean that the rider has to use them. They should not be used by the novice or any inexperienced rider: they should only be used for the re-training of problem horses.

Our horses do wear boots and bandages to protect them from knocks and bangs. It is questionable how much support they actu-

ally give to tendons and ligaments but I believe it is better to be safe than sorry.

Spurs are compulsory in international competitions and in some national competitions. They are not used to make a horse that is ignoring the leg aid more attentive. They are used as refinement and precision aids. We do not use them on our very young horses and I would never allow a rider who does not have a controlled and balanced seat to wear them. The size and length of the spur is determined by the length of the rider's leg and the shape of the horse. The severity of

subscribe to this as I have never considered the rest areas on busy highways and motorways to be safe enough places. I believe one should plan on shorter journeys with proper stable rest facilities available en route. It is important that there is an adequate supply of clean, sweet-smelling bedding available to soak up the urine and prevent contamination of the air quality.

To sum up, look after your dressage horse as you would any normal fit and precious competition horse. He requires vigilant supervision, constant consideration and a good understanding of stockmanship.

ABOVE LEFT
At international shows there is always much work to be done. Everyone must pull, or in this case, push his own weight!

ABOVE and BELOW
Monica Theodorescu takes a last-minute tack check before entering the arena, while Isabel Werth prefers to take something else! No, it isn't what it seems, alcohol is not allowed.

RIGHT
While the grooms remove Abner's bandages, his rider Mieke Lunskens, of Belgium, concentrates her thoughts on the test ahead.

the spur is determined by the overall ability of the person using them and the purpose for which they are used.

As far as whips are concerned, I carry a long dressage whip which I use for the bulk of the schooling. This means that I do not have to take my hand off the rein but, should the horse need further encouragement to listen to a leg, I can give him a sharp touch. I prefer the whip to be not too soft and not too thin as this can be painful.

With our very young horses, which have just been backed, I prefer to carry a well-made jumping whip. The whip must be used with consideration and very deliberately. I hate to see riders nagging on to their horses with schooling whips in what I would describe as a fly-swatting action. This only serves to irritate horses or make them so insensitive that even a bomb would not wake them.

In international competitions whips are not allowed; therefore, when my horses reach about the half-way point in their training I prefer to carry a whip only for short periods, when it is necessary, within a training session. In this way neither horse nor rider grow dependent on it.

The last piece of equipment that I do like my riders to wear are gloves. I feel that with leather schooling gloves the rider can achieve a nice firm contact on the rein which is most important.

Getting there

Finally, we start thinking about our competitions. We have to take into account transport. Horses are transported by road in either specialist horse trailers or horse boxes (horse transporters). The first concern is that they are thoughtfully driven, safe, serviced regularly and provided with good air flow and ventilation. An international trip may involve many hours of driving. We make a point of stopping every four hours to let the horse stretch his neck down and stretch his back muscles in order to prevent him from getting stiff.

On long hauls, some people recommend taking the horses off the transporter and giving them a leg stretch. I actually do not

CHAPTER
FOUR

The Way of Going –

Basic Aims and Essentials

So what exactly is dressage? I am sure you have been asked this particular question many times by the uninitiated yet interested enquirer. I simply reply that it is the training of the horse to make him more controllable, safe and pleasurable to ride. However, there is a point where this basic riding-horse requirement is replaced by sophisticated and more demanding techniques and this is where the sport of dressage, as we really know it, begins. From now on, the horse must work to his greatest gymnastic ability and mature into a well-muscled, supple and obedient equine athlete.

We have two parallel roads to travel: one is the route to increasing his physical

ABOVE and RIGHT
A four-year-old horse showing an active, swinging, working trot with supple back and (RIGHT) the finished product. Note the increased collection and weight carrying of the hind legs allowing for a lightened forehand. Keep this in mind as your target.

maturity, strength and dexterity to enable him to dance through the greatest demands of the Grand Prix test with apparent ease and effortlessness: the other must be to develop his mental understanding to enable him to perform a wide variety of exercises with confidence, willingness and honesty. These two paths are very much interlinked and dependent on one other.

For example, a weak horse will show an inability to perform a difficult movement by becoming tense and mentally upset. Likewise, it can be that a talented young horse has the physical ability in advance of a true understanding of a particular area. Think how often one sees a young horse, perhaps learning counter canter, but offering a flying change by mistake. Just because he can do it physically does not mean that he understands the complexities of the movement.

Priority points in understanding dressage

Now we are getting down to business, but let's also try and keep things clear and simple. What are the basic essentials that the judge is looking for?

The short answer is the correct execution of the required compulsory exercises, as laid down in the test paper, performed with correct and regular gaits and in the correct way of going.

I will discuss in later chapters the essentials of the gaits and the specific requirements of the exercises, but for now I should like to describe the 'jewel' of dressage competition riding, the way of going.

In order to establish a correct way of going we must identify the three fundamental components and understand the order of achievement and priority.

1 The first objective, before the subtleties of dressage can begin, is that the horse must instantly respond forward to the rider's leg signals. This is number one and takes priority over everything else. A car with an unreliable engine is not only tiresome but in certain instances dangerous. The same applies to riding horses, whatever their job.

I always say that the worst response is no response. The next worst is an adverse, or backward reaction to the rider's leg: but the best is an immediate forward and sensitive reaction to a light leg signal. Dressage is all about reproducing the exciting, fluent and graceful movements that we see the fresh horse perform when turned loose in his paddock. An unresponsive horse lacks the impetus for action and impulsion from which these natural movements emanate.

2 The second objective is to secure supple and loose back, body and neck muscles. This is achieved by tactful balanced riding, allowing ample time for the warming up and attention to general and specific suppling exercises. The horse will need to be suppled longitudinally, from his tail to his head, and also laterally to become equal to the left and the right. Like humans, most horses are more supple and coordinated to one side than the other. Correct training should endeavour to equal him up. This second objective will result in a round and soft outline.

I must point out here that some riders try to achieve this outline without spending time on the essential prerequisite of suppleness. It is not very difficult, by using 'trick' riding, to force the horse's head into a shape, but without the appreciation of elastic and supple muscles, any further training is pointless. It will result in underdeveloped, or incorrectly developed musculature, weakness, and possibly even unsoundness.

3 The third aim will, if the others have been achieved, almost look after itself. This aim is that the horse will accept a soft even contact, through the reins, to the rider's hands. The horse should not seek support, or lean on the rider's hands. The prime purpose of the rein contact is to establish a firm line of communication and to complete the

impulsion circuit which starts in the hind legs, travels over the horse's back, through the reins to the rider's hands and returns, via the rider's seat and legs back to the hindquarters.

With the responsiveness to the rider's leg and the suppleness of the horse's back, the rider will, by the use of the half halt (described in chapter 7) be able to encourage the horse's hind legs to step further underneath his body (engagement of the hindquarters) and carry some of the weight of his forehand onto his hind legs. When this happens the horse is said to be in self-carriage. He will not look to the reins for support and his whole forehand will lighten and adopt a relatively more 'uphill' direction. He will then be able to perform the competition exercises with lightness and ease. He will also feel confident and in harmony with his rider.

It is these combined qualities that make up the correct way of going that judges will expect to see demonstrated throughout the test. To emphasize their importance, they will not only be evaluated as the test progresses in the relevant place on the test sheet, they will also be summarized in the 'collective marks' at the end of the test. Each quality is categorized, and often receives a co-efficient, or multiplying factor, to stress its priority to the rider.

ABOVE and RIGHT
Nicole Uphoff-Becker and Rembrandt demonstrate the difference between training and the final presentation in the competition arena. Here we see Rembrandt being ridden 'deep' in order to stretch and supple his back muscles and later in the 'uphill' position with the poll, between the horse's ears, being the highest point.

BELOW
While Nicole concentrates here on longitudinal suppleness, Klaus Balkenhol works on lateral suppleness with lateral flexions. Note that he maintains a contact on the (outside) right rein even though the horse is flexed to the left.

BOVE and RIGHT
illian Davison and four-year-old No Limit work
rough two exercises to achieve confidence, freedom
id self-carriage.

29

Common Faults

Not going forward

Caused by lack of authority/effect from rider's legs or poor rein contact causing restriction. May be due to lack of understanding and sensitivity to rider's leg and seat aids. Can also be caused by nagging and ineffective leg aids; lack of correction in early stages. Pain/discomfort – stiff, tired, unfit horse. Improve precision, delivery and authority of leg aids. Be consistent and effective with correction.

Stiffness

Caused by unbalanced rider, incorrect past training or, most usually, incomplete warm up period before training session. Identify if stiffness is general or specific/local. Include more lateral work, possibly in walk, with varying degrees of flexion and bend. Consider working horse's top line forward and down, or in a deep position, while still encouraging hind legs to be engaged and active.

Lack of impulsion/flat

Caused by ineffective leg aids. Impulsion is contained energy – examine whether it is a lack of initial production or poor channelling of the impulsion. Stiffness or crookedness will interrupt the energy cycle which starts from the hind legs.

Not accepting bit, fussy mouth

May be due to unsteady rein contact from rider. Teeth, ill-fitting bit, stiffness in body/back, pain, discomfort are all possible causes. Mental tension and lack of confidence at the level of work being demanded of the horse are also possible causes which should be considered here.

Irregularity

When regularity of the sequence, or timing of the footfalls is broken. There can be many possible causes, including tension, lack of balance, stiffness, lack of impulsion and lameness.

Crookedness

When the hind legs do not follow in the tracks of the forelegs. Caused by rider not central in saddle, causing uneven rein and leg contact and effect. Stiffness, especially lateral, weakness, or pain are also possible causes. Most horses by nature are inclined to be crooked in canter, which is corrected by use of shoulder-in (see chapter 9).

WHEN READY TO START

The basic training of the horse should progressive and logical and taken step step according to the horse's physical a mental maturity. The horse will always learning, either the desirable way or t undesirable way, but he will always learning. Therefore, even with a very your horse, the trainer should start to channel t way of going in the right direction.

RIGHT
And finally the end product. Anky van Grunsven and Olympic Bonfire in a fantastic 'off the ground' extended canter. In spite of the slight opening of the horse's mouth, it is a wonderful example harmony c balance and power.

BELOW
Great Britian's Ferdi Eilberg on Arun Tor displays uphill balance due to the hindquarters carrying mo of the weight of the horse's forehand.

ABOVE
*Russia's Nina Menkova using controlled lateral
flexions to supple Dickson.*

LEFT
*Germany's Karin Rehbein taking care that this
extended trot on her impressive stallion Donerhall
does not give more front leg action than he is able to
match with his hind legs.*

CHAPTER
Five

The Rider's Effect

Imagine a dressage rider and the first picture your mind will probably conjure up is that of a long-legged, glamorously dressed, tall and elegant figure. However, when it comes to essential qualities I think the single most important one is an empathy, or understanding, with animals and, in particular, with horses. There is no question that some people are born more 'animal type' than others.

While I was lucky enough to be brought up with ponies and horses from a young age, an ever-increasing number of people these days enter the dressage sport with very little horse background. I believe that is essential to offer the dressage student general all-round equestrian education, s that they may become better horsemen an learn to understand how horses think an work and react.

The horse's mind dictates what his bod does. The dressage rider must therefore fir train his horse's mind. Influence throug effect and empathy are fundamental to th success of the dressage rider and trainer.

The effects of the riding position

Of course, we must all strive to achiev a better position and seat in the saddl as only a controlled and balanced sea allows us to deliver our signals to the hors with maximum ease and efficiency. Th rider's seat starts from the seat bones an like the stem of a young plant, the uppe body grows upwards and the leg positio grows downwards.

The suppleness of the rider's back i probably the most important technica quality in dressage riding. Any stiffnes in this area will result in a loss of balance unsteady legs and hands and stiffness in th horse's back. The rider's shoulders shoul sit square above supple loins and directl above the seat bones. The shoulders shoul at all times, be level and parallel to th ground. Furthermore, the rider's shoulder should always remain parallel to the horse' shoulders. This is especially importan to remember when riding circles and latera exercises.

From an erect but supple upper bod posture, the upper arms should hang softl down the sides with the elbow just in contac with the front part of the body. From here there should be a straight line from the rid er's elbow through the little finger, down th rein to the horse's bit. This direct straigh line should manifest itself when viewe from the side and also from a bird's ey point of view. Should the rider's hands b

carried too low, too high, too wide or too narrow, this will create an angle in the direction of the rein contact and will inhibit free communication.

Let us go back to the rider's base, the seat bones. Open and relaxed seat muscles should allow the legs to hang deeply down on either side of the horse. Avoid gripping with the thigh on the saddle flap. To encourage a deep lower leg position, allow your knees to relax down to the rear of the saddle flaps. The heels must be slightly lower than the toes because only a stretched calf muscle can deliver precise leg aids.

Remember the second plumb line which runs through the rider's ear, shoulder, hip and heel which helps achieve an upright and balanced position. These are, of course, only guidelines, as riders come in all different shapes and sizes with longer arms, and shorter legs: but the one essential is that they are independently balanced.

It is important that the rider learns to sit equally and centrally in the middle of the saddle. He should not only carry his arms and hands level, but also the angle and position of his legs should match from one side to the other. Beware of trying to force the toes too much to the front. On a narrow horse this can have the effect of taking the lower leg away from the horse's side, causing an unstable and inconsistent contact. When you get on the horse, do some leg stretching exercises to encourage your legs to stretch away and down and back with the thigh in contact but loose to the saddle flap.

Adapting to the shapes of horse and rider

We should take into account different shapes of horses and different shapes of riders with different lengths of legs when considering the actual leg position; always more important is the comfort and ease with which the rider sits and the effect and use of his legs, rather than the exact position. Never grip in with the knees, but allow the shape of the

ABOVE
The balanced seat. As a guide there should be a line through the rider's ear, shoulders and hip to heel, and another line from the rider's elbow, forearm, and rein to the bit.

LEFT
The rider's legs should hang in a natural, relaxed and comfortable position, in contact with the horse's sides. Avoid fixing the leg in a stiff, forced position as a slight variation will be necessary according to the different conformation of both horse and rider.

horse's rib cage to dictate the angle of your legs to his sides.

A broad horse, with a well sprung rib cage, will throw the back of the rider's thigh outwards and therefore give the effect of the rider's toes being more to the front and the foot being parallel to the horse. However, a narrow-girthed horse will require the rider's leg to be at a slight angle with the knees and the foot slightly pointing out in order that the rider's lower leg will make contact.

I mentioned before that suppleness is probably the single most technical quality that we should strive to improve as riders.

There is no doubt that some of us are naturally more pliant and flexible than others. Therefore, any exercises you can do dismounted to encourage your back and limbs to be free, lithe and strong will undoubtedly help with your seat. Only a supple and balanced rider will be able to feel with sensitivity what the horse is doing beneath him or interpret what the horse is about to do.

The signals we give are known as aids. We will be discussing more about aids for specific movements later on under individual chapters. The important point to remember is that individual horses react differently. There are lazy or cold types of horse which require sharper, more motivating signals and there are the more sensitive or hotter types that need much calmer, quieter aids.

Listen carefully to what the horse is saying

The rider must make an accurate assessment of what the horse requires at the different levels, stages and phases of training. He will take into account the mental reaction of the horse and must always interpret the horse's reply following a signal from the rider. Always listen carefully to what the horse is saying.

The cause of a particular reaction on the part of the horse is more important than the reaction itself. The first question to ask is, 'Is the horse physically strong enough to be able to perform this particular exercise? It could be that it is a young horse and not mature enough to fulfil the demands of a particularly strenuous exercise. At other times, it might be that we are doing this exercise too

late in the training session when the energy and impulsion levels are running out and the horse is already beginning to get muscle fatigue. If this should be the case, then obviously we must wait for another time in training when the horse is physically capable of carrying out what we require.

The second question to ask is, 'Does the horse understand what is required?' Just like teaching human beings we must strive for different ways of explaining to achieve comprehension. We must not be too narrow or limited in our training or our explanations of the exercises and must be prepared to take the lesson from a different angle.

The third question on our check list will be whether or not the horse is sufficiently interested or motivated to try to understand what we are asking. Beware the tone or atmosphere of the training session does not become dull, tedious and boring. If a horse's mind is not kept awake and interested, it should come as no great surprise if, when the trainer comes to a particular exercise, he finds that the horse's mind has switched off probably half an hour earlier.

We should always take into account that it is, in fact, the mind of the horse that we are training. Physically, it may be the horse's hind legs that we are trying to influence but what actually causes the horse's hind legs to move? It is an impulse, or signal, which originates in the horse's brain. So in our system of training we always train and work via this route.

We must be open-minded and discover different ways of motivating and influencing the horse. It is no good simply repeating the same thing or – rather like the Englishman abroad – merely shouting louder. Especially when we introduce new work, or when we run into difficulties, we should be prepared to try a different language or explanation route, in order to secure the required reaction. After this, we will then be able to establish the basis for an agreed communication system of aids and signals to lead us forward.

CHAPTER
SIX
Walk, Trot and Canter

The walk, trot and canter are known as the gaits, or paces, of the horse. In each of the gaits the horse moves his legs in a different sequence and therefore each gait has its own rhythm. If the training and riding has been correct, the gaits given by nature to the horse at birth will remain correct and regular in rhythm and display expression and pride. It is essential that we should examine the important qualities of each gait.

The Walk

To the spectator, and sometimes even to some riders, the walk appears to be the least exciting pace. It can easily be ignored while riders concentrate on the more fascinating movements of the trot and canter. However, our responsibility covers all three gaits and to encourage adequate attention to these important aspects, many tests multiply part of the walk 'total'.

Thus, by competing a horse with a spoilt, or undeveloped walk, the loss of potential marks can be expensive in terms of both results and prizes. Furthermore, from a training angle, the walk may be used for teaching and explaining new exercises, especially lateral work, as it is easier for the rider to maintain balance and thus deliver more exact aids and signals.

The Collected Walk

Because the horse will be taking more weight on the hind legs, his steps will be shorter. It is important that activity in the collected walk encourages the horse to bend the joints of each leg noticeably and equally. Most horses in collected walk usually under-track. This means that the imprint of the horse's hind foot does not quite reach the track left by the foreleg on the same side.

Young, or novice horses, should not be asked to perform collected walk.

Medium Walk

This is the middle gear when the horse usually overtracks. It is the walk most often used, and the mode of walk in which all young horses will begin their training. It is usually omitted from the more advanced tests.

Extended Walk

This is when the horse gains as much ground as possible with each step. His neck should be lengthened, yet he should remain on the bit and rein contact with the rider's hand maintained. In extended walk the horse should really march forward without losing rhythm or hurrying.

Free Walk on a Long Rein

This is similar to an extended walk but the rider gives the rein to the point where no contact is maintained and the horse has complete freedom of his head and neck.

In training, it is used during rest periods or as a reward. For competition purposes it is used for younger horses or at the completion of every international test when the horse leaves the arena.

The Walk – Priority Points

What it is

A pace of four-time. There are four beats to one stride. The sequence being: near hind, near fore, off hind, off fore. Variations: medium, collected, extended and free walk. There is no moment of suspension in the walk sequence.

Aim/Look for

Correct way of going (page 29).

Four equally spaced beats.

Active and purposeful, yet calm.

Correct mode (collected, medium etc.)

LEFT
Notice how far underneath his body Goldstern engages his hind leg. He is therefore able to spring expressively forwards and upwards into the air with a light forehand. Both horse and rider are superbly balanced.

ABOVE
A young horse performing medium walk with four clear beats.

Common Faults

Specific faults other than those affecting basic way of going.

Irregular rhythm

Loss of four equally spaced beats. Almost/actually pacing, that is, moves legs together on the same side. Probably the most serious fault. Mostly caused by stiffness in the horse's body, mental tension, drawing back and resistance in the mouth and neck. The rider using a rough rein contact or collecting the horse from in front instead of behind will often cause this.

Correction: identify cause and improve. In medium walk achieve an established and correct way of going and then gradually collect and/or extend. Use the medium walk as a base.

Walk becomes too slow in rhythm instead of collecting

Most often caused by the rider's misinterpretation of collection. May also be caused by a lack of activity.

Steps too short, not covering enough ground especially in extended

Caused by the natural walk lacking freedom, otherwise rider-induced. Encourage and allow more freedom by securing downward stretch of the horse's neck. Ask horse to walk more actively from the hind legs and over the back. Vary and experiment with different type of leg aids.

Note

Under and overtracking are only a guide as to the relative length of the walk steps. Each horse has his own natural size of step, and greater importance should be placed on the relative difference and correctness rather than merely the overtrack.

RIGHT
An active and extremely collected walk. The horse is ready for anything that may be asked of him.

BELOW
Note the different outline in this extended walk, compared to the collected walk opposite. The horse's neck is encouraged to stretch forward to enable him to take longer steps. However, he still maintains a rein contact and is on the bit.

The Trot

The trot, especially the working trot, is probably the most often used pace. Because it is almost symmetrical in the sequence of movement, it is easier to balance than the canter yet offers more impulsion and forwardness than the walk.

Common Faults

Specific faults other than those affecting basic way of going.

On the forehand

Caused by lack of activity, engagement and weight carrying on the hind legs.

Correction: use the half halt, which is an extremely effective way to rebalance horse. (See Chapter 7).

Stiff back

Caused by inadequate warming up, or stiffness in the rider's back, especially in the sitting trot.

Correction: incorporate more suppling exercises during warming up, such as circles, serpentines, and lateral work in walk.

Broken diagonal

This is where the hind foot touches down first. It is often seen in extended trot where the elevation of the forehand is not a true consequence of the hindquarters taking more weight but, instead, of a heightening of the forehand often by too much use of the hands and the curb of the double bridle.

Correction: allow slight lengthening and lowering of the horse's neck, whilst still maintaining balance, in order to free and loosen the back muscles.

The Trot – Priority Points

What it is

A pace of two-time. The horse moves in diagonal pairs with an important movement of suspension, when all four legs are off the ground.

There are four modes of trot:- working (the basis of the trot works for young or novice horses. It is also used for warming up and cooling down older, more experienced horses).

The other three are collected, medium and extended.

Aim/Look for

Correct way of going (page 29).

Uphill balance.

Active hind leg stepping energetically under the horse's body.

Supple top line 'over the back and on the bit'.

Correct type/mode i.e. collected, extended etc.

RIGHT
Here Rembrandt is springing off his hind legs into a well-cadenced extended trot. The dimension of the trot and the moment of suspension are very clear. The horse is impressively off the ground and uphill due to the well-engaged hindquarters.

LEFT
The working trot is used for young horses. The hind legs should swing well underneath the horse's body, but are not expected to carry as much weight as in collected trot. This horse is being ridden in a slightly deep outline into the rein contact. Before the test he would need to come up in the poll.

The Canter

The canter is perhaps the most important gait for the advanced competition horse. For example, at Grand Prix level, many marks are awarded for the intricate test of the flying changes every stride, the full canter pirouettes and the counter change of hand as well as the usual exercises of extended canter and the transitions in between. The horse with an inherently weak canter, or spoilt by training, can never receive good marks, no matter how accurately the exercises are performed.

ABOVE
A younger horse in counter canter. This is where the horse canters in outside lead. It is a useful straightening and control exercise, but like all exercises should be introduced progressively, starting with loops off the long side, small half circles returning to the track halfway down the long side and maintaining counter canter until the first corner. Later, the horse may be asked to keep the counter canter through the first and second corners and eventually strike off directly into counter canter. Notice how the quality of the canter is maintained with the horse's weight carried on the hind legs.

The Vital Canter – Priority Points

What it is

A pace of three-time. In the right lead canter, the sequence is initiated with the left hind leg touching the ground first, followed by the diagonal pair of the right hind leg and left front leg and then the leading foreleg.

This sequence of leg movements is then followed by the important moment of suspension, when all four legs are off the ground at the same time. As with the trot, there are four variations of canter: working, used for establishing the early training work and warming up, collected, medium and extended.

Aim/look for
Correct way of going (page 29).

Correct three beat sequence.

Clear and expressive moment of suspension.

Ability to transfer the weight back on well-flexed hind legs.

Nice height to the front leg reaction through a well-bent knee joint.

Appropriate type/mode i.e. collected, extended etc.

Common Faults

Steps flat, lacking spring off ground

Balance is down on the forehand, often when the horse appears long and flat. Use half halts on a circle to encourage the horse to take more weight back on the hind legs. As you reduce the length of stride also increase the height. To maintain motivation make sharp transitions from working canter to medium canter. When in medium canter, do not allow the horse's body to sprawl longer; instead, keep him shorter in the frame but springing boldly through the air.

Four-time canter

Rhythm is broken due to lack of attention to moment of suspension or lack of scope in the natural canter. May be caused by too much rein and too little leg effect. Often appears when attempting to increase collection in canter.

Correction: return to good working canter and make sharp transitions to medium. When collecting canter, do this more gradually and only for a few strides at a time before returning to working or medium.

On forehand, croup high

Maybe natural conformation predisposes the horse to being croup high. Nevertheless, ensure that when half halting, the horse actually transfers a small amount of weight back.

Correction: use gradual canter half pass and big working pirouettes to encourage the horse at least to become level between croup and withers and then later to slightly lower croup. Encourage this improved technique to be reproduced in the normal collected canter.

Crooked

In young horses, a certain amount of crookedness is natural in canter. However, this needs to be corrected if long-term chronic wear and tear are to be avoided.

The horse should always be straightened in canter by placing his forehand in front of his quarters. This means we can only really straighten the horse when he understands shoulder-in, first in trot and later, more specifically, in canter. Therefore, do not attempt to straighten the canter before this point. Too much straightening of a young horse's canter too early in his training can cause tension and restriction.

Before attempting to straighten the canter by use of shoulder-in (see diagram on page 55), use the outside rein to ensure that the horse does not have too much neck bend which will predispose him to go into shoulder-out. This fault must be corrected before the horse's shoulders are brought in. Only maintain for a few strides at first and then later extend the number of strides.

Horses schooled for long periods in an enclosed area against a fence or a wall are inclined to line up their outside shoulder against the fence and use this as a support. The bird's eye view of the arrowhead formation thus becomes lopsided and the use of impulsion inefficient. Therefore, great attention at the appropriate time should be paid to progressively straightening the horse. It is essential that when the horse canters on circular lines, he should be correctly bent in his body, yet his hind feet should continue to track straight into the corresponding fore feet. Always check, too, that the rider is sitting straight and central in the saddle for it is only a straight rider who can develop a straight horse.

ABOVE
If you try to emulate horse and rider in this picture of the extended canter, you won't go far wrong!

CHAPTER
SEVEN

The Half Halt –

The Punctuation of the Dressage Horse

The half halt is the most important technique and the most often-used exercise in dressage. It links and coordinates all the essential ingredients – suppleness, balance, impulsion, rhythm and bend.

To understand why it is so important, it is necessary for us to take a look at the natural balance and weight distribution of the horse's conformation. If God had not given the horse a long neck and heavy head on the front end he would be left with a leg at each corner and be as well-balanced and secure as your kitchen table. Without such a neck it would be difficult to imagine how our horse could engage in his favourite pastime – eating grass! Thus, the secure 'kitchen table' balance of the horse is disturbed by this extra weight on one end and he has been given, by nature, more weight on the forelegs than on the hind legs.

The progressive training of the horse therefore aims to encourage the horse's hind legs to step further underneath towards the centre of balance and thus relieve the front legs of some of the load.

Our first aim in training is to encourage the horse's hind legs to take sufficient weight so that there is equal weight bearing between the front legs and the hind legs and the horse comes into a horizontal balance. This level of collection is expected at the medium level training of the horse. Later, when the horse becomes stronger and more educated, we will see how the hind legs step even more underneath, so that they adopt a slight sitting appearance and are responsible for more weight on the hind legs than there is on the front legs. When this happens the forehand is extremely light and the horse is in total self-carriage. It is like having power steering.

Imagine that we could perform our dressage at the halt once we had balanced the horse at the beginning of the training session, and assuming he remained stationary; then the balance would stay constant. However, dressage is all about movement, and because balance is a fluid state it is necessary to rebalance in an instant. The only way of doing this is by understanding and mastering the half halt technique.

In simple terms, a half halt persuades the horse's forehand and front legs to wait

while the hind legs catch up and step once again underneath the horse's body. We establish this exercise in the following progression:

In halt, the rider uses small, quick leg aids in a varied rhythm to encourage the hind feet to step slightly more under and towards the front feet. This also encourages the horse to become what we call 'over and through the back, into the rein contact and in self carriage'.

The next stage is to make walk, halt, walk transitions, again asking for the horse's hind legs to step squarely underneath. You will probably notice at this stage that as the young horse halts he leaves one particular hind leg slightly further out to the rear than the other. To encourage him to step forward with that hind leg, use your leg on the same side. Sometimes, instead of just taking a half step forward with the offending leg, the horse takes a full step and goes from leaving it out the back to stepping too far underneath. This is by far preferable to a horse that learns to half square but with too much distance between the front feet

and the hind feet, so that he is with both hind legs still out the back.

Progress to trot, halt, trot transitions, being consistent in the way you encourage him to step underneath with the hind legs.

Soon you will be able to reduce your full halts into a momentary pause in the movement while the hind legs catch up. And now you are doing half halts.

As with every exercise, it is important to observe and assess whether the horse is performing and reacting correctly during this particular exercise. Always remember the purpose: to encourage the hind legs to step further under the body and nearer the front legs. We must discourage any tendency to restrict the neck or the forelegs of the horse. It is not a question of bringing the front legs backwards and head in but quite the opposite. The idea is to bring the hind legs forward underneath the horse's body.

The coordination between the rider's legs, seat and hands is vital and requires constant fine tuning. Beware of merely checking the pace; in other words, slowing down and losing impulsion, with the hind

legs still staying too far away from the horse's centre of balance. This may give the impression of greater control but it cannot be considered a correctly executed half halt and it therefore offers limited value.

Now we can see what an essential linking tool the half halt is. The half halt is the connecting link, or punctuation of dressage.

ABOVE

Andiamo and Sven Rothenberger. Although Sven now rides for Holland, he previously rode for Germany and won many top competitions on this horse. The half halt is the link between balance and impulsion and the means by which skilled dressage riders prepare and communicate, almost invisibly, with their horses. Unsightly hand action or interruption of the rhythm flow is not the objective. Here we see good balance and harmony.

CHAPTER
EIGHT

Single Track Work

 W hy is it that even when one is watching a Grand Prix test one seldom sees correctly ridden corners? Very rarely does the horse show correct and even bend through the corners, equal in both directions. Instead, one sees impressive movements, extensions, half passes and other advanced movements, but the single track work of corners and small circles and turns across the school and on to the diagonal and up the centre line are often less than good. It seems very strange to me, because every trainer that I know will tell you that this basic work is, in fact, the most important.

I pay a lot of attention to accuracy. I insist that when my riders are schooling and training their horses they only ever make a circle at a marker and that the circle size should always be predetermined. It is all too easy when you are schooling to think, 'Oh, I will just put in a circle here', and then the size of the circle just happens to be what is given. But this does not help to develop that part of our brain which copes with accurate, predetermined movements.

I spend a lot of time making sure that not only are the circles accurate in size and placed correctly at the marker with the marker opposite to the centre of the circle, but also that we use the circles to develop greater suppleness and evenness of bend. After all, the reason circles are included in dressage tests is to prove or demonstrate suppleness.

Turns

A turn is simply a quarter of a circle. We have turns on to the centre line, across the school on the EB line and, of course, in every corner of the arena. Like circles, turns should be ridden to a predetermined size. In principle, a large turn is a quarter of a 10-metre circle, and a small turn for an advanced horse is equal to a quarter of a 6-metre circle.

In my school, I chalk up on the walls the distances from the corner of the school to the 3-metre points which coincide with the 6-metre circle and the 5-metre points which correspond to a quarter of the 10-metre circle. I make each rider excute every single turn or corner in the school as an individual exercise. I insist that they prepare correctly before the corner, perhaps riding a very small angle of shoulder-in to help get the horse round the inside leg to the outside rein; with horses that are stiff through the turns and throw their quarters out, they might even ride a little bit of quarters-in or travers (see page 55) to help prevent the (hind) quarters of the horse going to the outside.

To re-emphasize the point, I feel that corners are the foundation of correct, accurate dressage riding. They are included in every test from the novice horse to the Grand Prix and it isn't until I start really riding corners that I feel that I am 'in the groove' on a particular day. For me, they are the Number One exercise.

Progressing on from the corners in the school, we have the turns up the centre line or across the school where obviously you don't have a right-angle of dressage boards or a fence to help you. This is where you have to have the horse correctly centred on the aids to make sure that he follows an even and predetermined line to take him smoothly through the turn with minimum loss of balance, rhythm or impulsion.

Centre Lines

A lot of riders get their priorities wrong when training a young horse on the centre line. The

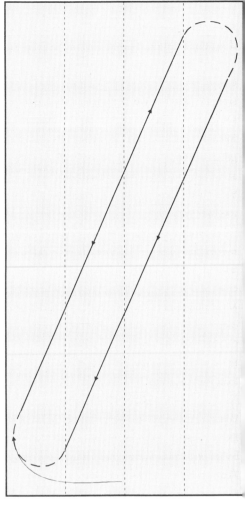

K

first priority is not whether the horse is straight, but whether he is in front of the leg, through the back to a supple poll and into an even contact, and taking us forward down the centre line.

Generally, the centre line is not used enough in our daily work, and in training sessions I insist that, on certain days, we only change the rein down the centre line. The aim is to reproduce the same feel as if you are riding down the long side, or in any other movement and to have the same priorities. Then the horse becomes automatically straight. Beware of 'fiddling' straightness, but ensure that it is the result of suppleness and engagement.

The horse's hind legs must be correctly underneath him if the transitions into and out of halt and the turn at C are to succeed. Lack of engagement is reflected in poor transitions and one should remember that it will also be reflected in the judges' marks!

Turning on to the diagonal

Here again, I insist that riders ride the turns absolutely correctly, completing the turn well before the marker, then going a little bit straight and turning on to a really clean, straight diagonal line.

We practise all these turns individually to ensure that there is no loss of rhythm or impulsion, for later on we will be including into this some steps of medium trot on the diagonal. It follows that if the horse is unbalanced or struggling through the turn, he is hardly likely to arrive on the diagonal with sufficient quality to be able to spring into a correctly executed medium trot.

I actually use a number of diagonal lines in my training programme, as we will be seeing later on with some of the more advanced exercises, and instead of just using, for example, the KXM diagonal of the school, I sometimes use a diagonal line from K to the centre line marker at C. This has many of advantages, its main one in this context being that it makes the rider actually look for the marker.

Rein Back

When it comes to teaching the rein back, I first like a horse to have been accustomed to going backwards from the voice aid without the rider. That might involve teaching him, for instance, in the stable or even in the school dismounted. I put one hand on the reins and the other hand on his chest, give him a little pat or tap on the chest, using the voice at the same time, and just get him moving forwards and back freely and easily.

Initially, I do not fuss him about being straight in the rein back. Straightening up comes later. I am more concerned at this stage that he goes back freely and willingly.

Later on, under saddle, when it is time to straighten him up, I very often go into a small shoulder-in angle and, halting by the wall of the arena, ask him to go back. The shoulder-fore angle normally counteracts the tendency for the hindquarters to come in. If this isn't enough, then with the schooling whip on that side and a little use of the leg, I gradually teach his quarters to stay on the track. But I only ever concentrate on straightening when the horse is going freely back from the voice.

The last stage of the rein back is to keep your legs in the slightly more forward driving influence as the horse is actually going back so that he keeps his hind legs underneath him even though he is stepping backwards. All too often you see horses rushing back or even the

opposite, reluctantly dragging backwards on their forehands and with their heads down. This is because the hind legs are still not underneath the horse and carrying the forehand. With an advanced horse it is quite easy to encourage him to keep the hind legs underneath and connected whilst he steps backwards.

LEFT
Riding a supple horse straight. Practising the centre line and halt. The rider is patting the horse as a reward.

DIAGRAM
An exercise I call parallel diagonal lines. It is particularly useful for keeping young horses balanced and straight when cantering across the diagonal. Later on, by riding travers through the half circles at the end, it can be used for working canter pirouettes. (See page 66).

ABOVE
The way of going we're all aiming for!

CHAPTER
NINE

Going Sideways

'Do not measure your progress by the movements you make but by "how" you make them.'

Leg Yielding – Priority Points

What it is

When the horse moves forward and sideways more or less straight in his body from tail to poll. It can be done in walk, trot and canter.

It need not be done in a collected pace and is therefore useful for young horses, or older, stiffer horses not yet supple enough for collected.

It is useful exercise to develop the novice rider's coordination in lateral work.

It is the first preliminary lateral exercise.

Aim/Look for

Correct way of going (page 29)

The horse remaining parallel to the long side of the arena.

An instant and sensitive reaction to a right leg aid.

The horse seeking a steady rein contact, especially in the opposite rein to the sideways asking leg. Thus the horse comes on to the diagonal aids.

Measured and balanced steps.

The lateral movements, or sideways exercises, used in international tests are shoulder-in and half pass. However, there are other exercises, such as leg yielding travers and renvers, that we use in training.

In the trot and the canter the horse moves sideways during the moment of suspension when all four legs are off the ground. Therefore, it follows that the more gymnastic the way of going, that is, the higher the horse comes off the ground, the easier it is for him to move sideways.

Priority Point

Use for leg response and control purposes. Never allow excessive neck bend as this causes the horse to **fall** sideways through the shoulders.

Common Faults

Specific faults other than those affecting basic way of going

The horse falls through the outside shoulders and loses lateral balance

Correction: maintain better outside rein contact. Make angle less acute. (See page 65).

The horse does not move sideways enough

Correction: use sharper, quicker leg aids reinforced with schooling whip. Do not progress to trot until horse is more sensitive in walk. (See page 65).

WHEN TO START

Almost immediately, providing the horse responds to the forward driving aids.

PROGRESSION

1 In walk, from inside track or a line, complete turn, ride straight then ask for controlled forward and sideways steps until reaching the outside track. Repeat in trot.

2 Leg yielding away from the wall towards the quarter or centre line.

3 Use on short side of arena to teach horse to go into corner.

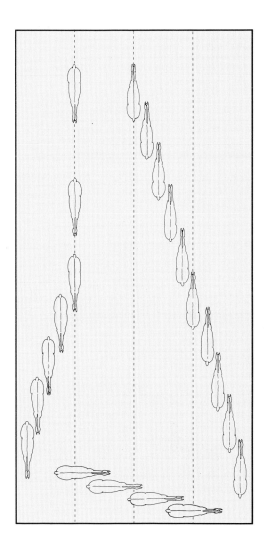

DIAGRAM
Leg yielding is a basic exercise to establish leg response. On the left, the horse is asked to perform the first stage of leg yielding from the quarter line towards the outside track, towards which young horses are naturally attracted. Later, as on the right, the horse must also learn to leave the track by leg yielding towards the centre line.

The diagram also shows leg yielding on the short side which helps to encourage the horse into the corner.

OPPOSITE
Carol Lavell and the amazingly loose-jointed Gifted. This horse has a fantastic ability to cross and float across the arena in his half passes.

LEFT
Nicole Uphoff-Becker and Rembrandt in half pass. The basis of all good lateral work is the horse's instant response to the rider's leg aids in both sideways and forwards direction. Although he may be moving sideways from one leg, the horse must also respond immediately to the rider's opposite leg. Thus the angle and way of going is maintained.

Shoulder-in – purpose

To encourage the hind legs to step under and carry more of the weight off the forehand. It also supples and achieves greater control of the shoulders and thus facilitates straightness. Particularly useful for straightening up the canter.

Common Faults

Too much neck bend and no angle

To correct this, in walk, encourage small angle with straight neck, or even outside flexion if necessary, until outside foreleg steps in off the track. Progress to trot later. Re-introduce bend gradually.

Too much angle and no bend

Walk, and later trot down track with only small degree of flexion, and no angle. When greater lateral suppleness is achieved gradually re-introduce angle but maintain bend.

Quarter-out, rather than forehand-in

Maintain better, more effective outside leg. For older horses, use travers. Start when horse executing leg yielding easily.

BUILD-UP EXERCISES

1 In walk, perform leg yielding diagonally against wall. Ask for only a few steps and then exit the exercise by either:

A) Circling away from exercise if the horse was reluctant to offer angle; or

B) Going straight down track if the horse was inclined to give too much angle.

2 Maintain shoulder-in for more steps. Always be able to ride at least two different angles, using the small one to establish a fluent and easy rhythm. A small angle of shoulder-in is known as a shoulder-fore.

Priority Point

It is always better to ride a small angle and maintain good balance and control.

Shoulder-in – Priority Points

What it is

Where the horse travels with his hind legs on the outside track and his front legs on the inside track. He is bent, evenly, away from the direction in which he is travelling.

Aim/Look for

Correct way of going (page 29).

A consistent angle of about 30 degrees.

Fluent and regular rhythm.

Uphill balance.

Regular and even lead.

Equal lateral balance.

TOP RIGHT
A shoulder to the fore is a useful straightening and suppling training exercise.

RIGHT
A young horse in shoulder-in. Although there could be more bend through the horse's body, note the good contact on the (outside)right rein.

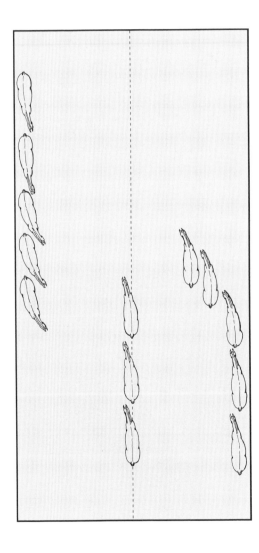

DIAGRAM
The difference in angle between the training exercise of shoulder-fore and a competition shoulder-in. Note how the shoulder-fore may be used to straighten the canter, shown here on the centre line and, on the right as a preparation before departing into half pass. In a competition, however, the angle must be consistent.

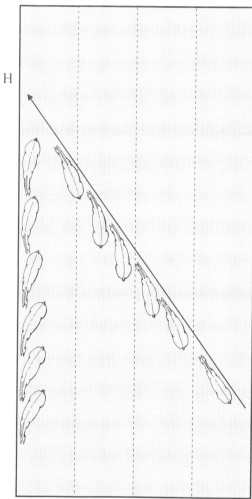

Too much angle
Use less outside leg and more inside leg.

Not enough bend
Happens when horse offers too much angle. In walk, establish flexion and bend before asking the quarters to step in slightly.

Horse drifting in from track
Relax outside leg aid, momentarily, and use inside leg more to encourage the horse to step forward towards outside track.

BUILD-UP EXERCISES

1   Start after shoulder-in established. Against wall, in walk, or even halt, ask hind legs to step slightly in. Do not worry about bend at this stage.

2   Maintain for more steps.

3   Once hind legs are under control add small but even bend while maintaining good outside rein contact.

4   Progress into trotting through exercises.

DIAGRAM
Variations in angle of travers on the long side and on the diagonal. A useful exercise to encourage flow and control in the half pass and heighten the rider's awareness of the positioning of the hindquarters in relation to the forehand.

ABOVE LEFT
A small angle of travers done, on this occasion, along the diagonal. This helps achieve fluency later on in half pass. Always keep your shoulders parallel to the horse's and in the direction of the movement.

CHAPTER
TEN

Half Pass

Everybody enjoys watching a lovely flowing half pass, the horse gliding effortlessly from one side of the arena to the other. But how are these movements achieved? Are the horses on well-oiled casters, and how do they cross legs so easily?

Let's look at the requirements and necessary components for riding good half passes.

Common Faults

Specific faults other than those affecting basic way of going.

Too much neck bend

Use outside rein to reduce neck bend. Do not pull on inside rein.

Lack of bend

Can be due to angle becoming too acute. Practise flexion exercises, then re-introduce to gradual angle.

Hindquarters trailing

Due to lack of response to outside leg. Use travers. Incorporate a few steps of half pass and come out in travers. Be sure the problem is not due to the forehand being out of control and falling sideways in advance of the hindquarters.

Hindquarters leading

Due to too much outside leg and not enough inside leg. Can be due to bad presentation at start, use shoulder-fore before and at end of half pass.

Loss of regularity and impulsion

Mostly due to angle being too acute and horse dropping behind the rider's inside leg. Ensure that the horse is in good quality collection before commencing half pass and then make angle more gradual. Very often riders start the movement late and finish early, thus increasing the angle and difficulty of the half pass.

Not going sideways

The pace is earth bound and lacking spring. Also caused by the preliminary exercises not being good enough. Suggested exercise as follows. Leg yielding, into half pass and then finishing again in leg yielding, all in the same direction. The aim of this exercise is to make the horse more sensitive and responsive to the sideways leg aids. (See page 53, leg yielding).

WHEN READY TO START

After leg yielding, shoulder-in and travers are established.

BUILD UP

1 Leg yielding from the outside track.

2 Shoulder-fore down long side.

3 Travers down the long side.

PROGRESSION EXERCISE

1 On the long side, ride a few steps of shoulder-fore into half pass. When you reach the quarter line ride straight. Repeat until fluent in both directions. Start in walk, then progress on to trot.

2 Use travers across diagonal to ensure relative placing of the hindquarters and forehand. This helps achieve easy flowing steps.

3 Turn down the centre line. As always, establish a shoulder-fore and then into half pass. Always remember to finish the turn and prepare the forehand and then depart gradually into half pass.

4 In the middle section of a half pass, ask the horse to travel more sideways. Always keep the first and last steps more forward and gradual.

5 Pay great attention to the beginning and the end. Remember, you can always tell how tidy a rider's bedroom is by the way they start and finish their half pass! However, in

LEFT
Kyra Kyrkland of Finland and Edinburgh sweep across the practice arena in a good half pass to the right.

BELOW
Canter half pass to the left. The horse's body is almost parallel to the long side of the arena, bent correctly into the direction of the movement with the forehand correctly placed very slightly in advance of the hind legs. The rider's position is excellent – upright and central in the saddle, with his shoulders parallel to the horse's.

training you can always alter the end of a half pass according to the faults being offered. For example, if the horse is trailing with the hindquarters, finish sometimes in a travers position. However, do not forget to return to the normal execution of the half pass exercise.

6 When fluent in trot, start to build up again at step 1 in canter. On the outside track, from shoulder-fore position, ride three to four strides of canter half pass to the quarter line and then ride straight. Repeat on both reins.

7 Repeat in canter as per trot progression.

Counter Change of Hand – Priority Points

What it is

Where the horse performs a half pass in one direction followed immediately by a half pass in the other direction. There may be five or six consecutive changes of direction and it can be performed in trot and canter. When performed in trot, the horse is required to travel a given number of metres either side of the centre line. However, in canter, the half passes are measured by the number of strides either side of the centre line with flying changes in between each half pass.

Aim/Look for

Correct way of going (page 29).

Correctness of each half pass technique – bend, almost parallel etc.

Even distance travelled each way.

When performed in canter, correct number of strides and correctness and quality of flying changes.

Controlled straight beginning and end to exercise.

Common Faults

Incorrect half passes i.e. quarters leading/trailing

Caused by lack of control during preparation and changeover. Always ride straight and achieve shoulder-fore before starting the new half pass.

Not centrally placed

Caused by inaccurate riding and the horse lacking equal sideways fluency (P. 57: Half Pass). In the short term, the rule is only to allow the horse to travel as much sideways as he can manage in the difficult direction.

Losing balance and going on to forehand

Probably going too much sideways. Use the straight strides in between each half pass to re-engage and balance.

Incorrect number of canter strides

Caused by lack of control and preparation on rider's part.

Short, flat, flying changes

Use two straight strides before each change and improve quality of canter before change.

WHEN READY TO START

When trot and canter half passes and flying changes are established.

BUILD UP

When practising half passes:

1 Be particularly careful to finish each one directly and straight.

2 Ride a trot half pass to the centre line, ride straight and develop shoulder-fore in the opposite direction.

3 In canter, ride some strides of a half pass – two strides straight – flying change – shoulder-fore – straight.

4 When riding a canter half pass, get into the habit of counting the number of strides.

5 Practise varying the amount sideways within each half pass so that the horse is flexible and responsive according to where you want to place him.

STEPS AND PROGRESSION

1 In trot from the long side, shoulder-fore – half pass to the quarter line straight line – straight – shoulder-fore in the opposite direction – half pass back to the track.

2 Practise using the halfway line EB in order to centralize the exercise.

3 Note in which direction the horse is less fluent and let this dictate how far sideways you travel initially.

4 Repeat the above exercises to and from different lines, e.g. quarter line, three-quarter line and centre line.

5 In canter, practise the build-up exercise from the long side, half pass until the quarter line – two strides straight – flying change – shoulder-fore in the opposite direction until the end of the school.

Then turn in counter canter and turn on to the three-quarter line. Present the horse into shoulder-fore and half pass to the track – two strides straight – flying change – ride straight. Make a note of the number of half pass strides and try to make each one match.

6 Putting two half passes together. From the outside track, canter six strides of half pass – two strides straight – flying change – shoulder-fore one stride – then half pass back to the track, allowing one stride straight before another flying change.

7 Repeat the exercise using different lines. Always use the EB line as the half-way guide point.

8 When flowing and controlling equally to and from a definite line, try going equally either side of the centre line.

Priority Point

Always go straight in between each half pass in order to re-engage, control and prepare for the new half pass. Centre the exercise by gauging the sideways flow and using the EB line as your halfway mark.

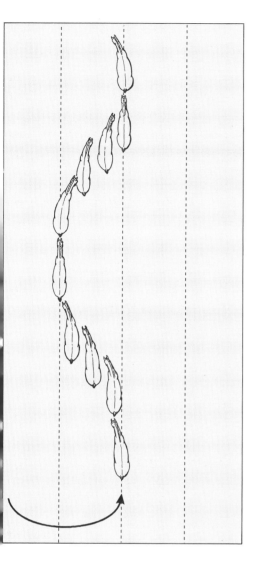

RIGHT

How you finish one half pass determines the control you will have at the start of the next! Here the rider has correctly moved the hindquarters directly behind the forehand, thus making the horse virtually parallel to the long side of the arena and is beginning to straighten the horse ready for a flying change. Precision is the priority in half passes and the foundation for the counter change of hand.

DIAGRAM

A counter change of hand is all about refined control allowing the correct placing of the horse's hindquarters and the forehand. This training exercise incorporates the basis of the simple counter change. The horse is asked to half pass from the centre line to the quarter line and back again. The quarter and three-quarter lines are important guide lines for accurate exercises.

LEFT

As a training exercise, the rider has moved this young horse's forehand clearly in advance of the hindquarters in this left half pass. This encourages freedom of the shoulders but if performed in a competition may lose marks for the hindquarters trailing.

CHAPTER
ELEVEN
Flying Changes

Flying changes, which in tests are performed individually or in a sequence, are always very exciting to ride and, when performed with gymnastic expression, also most attractive to watch. They are probably the first real obstacle we have to face in our dressage training. All horses vary in how easily and quickly they progress through them, but it is always a relief when they become established.

Flying Changes – Priority Points

What they are

When the horse changes from one lead canter to the other in a single moment of suspension. Flying changes are performed individually or in a sequence, often called 'tempo changes.' At Prix St. George, changes every four and three strides are required, Intermediare I every three and two strides, while at the highest standard, Grand Prix, changes every second and every stride, called one-time changes, are required.

Aim/Look for

Correct way of going (page 29).

Horse must change front legs and hind legs at the same time, in the same moment of suspension.

During the flying change, the horse should spring expressively off the ground.

The uphill balance of the horse should be maintained. However, in order to encourage big forward changes, the collection is allowed slightly more freedom.

In tempo changes, the correct number of changes and the correct number of strides in between each change must be performed.

The horse must do straight changes on a straight line. The changes must be accurately placed at the given marker or spaced evenly across the diagonal line. The rider's signals should be almost imperceptible but the horse should react immediately to the aid.

Common Faults

The horse changes first with the front legs and later behind. Known as being late behind

Caused by canter too long and flat or horse disturbed by, and not understanding, aids.

Improve control, quality and spring of canter. Try more subtle aid and different place in school or some half pass strides just before asking.

The horse changes with the hind legs first, known as being early behind

This is usually caused because the horse is too much on forehand at moment of change or the horse changes bend before completing flying change, thus restricting freedom of new inside foreleg moving through.

Improve balance in canter and lighten forehand. Ensure rider not allowing or encouraging the horse to change neck bend before change. Always keep horse straight on the new outside rein.

The horse is late to the rider's signals

Incorrect preparation and delivery of aids. Increase spring in canter as approach will warn horse of impending change. Use more precise, sharper leg aid, possibly reinforced by a touch of the schooling whip, if necessary.

Flat changes, lacking expression

Inadequate canter, lacking spring and athleticism.

LEFT and ABOVE
The novice and the master! Although there is a slight loss of balance while this young horse makes a flying change, both horses display the uphill direction and expressive canter vital for good flying changes.

suading the horse to perform the exercise fc
himself and to his own advantage, even
initially he considers it an escape or evasior

WHEN HORSE READY TO STAR

Often, young horses offer a flying chang
perhaps due to a lack of balance or a
an escape from early exercises in count
canter. In this situation, and with the futur
in mind, as long as these changes are corre
and not late behind, I never punish the hors
but simply walk and strike off again int
counter canter.

I normally start to work on changes afte
the horse is balanced in counter canter, ca
be straightened with a small angle of cant
shoulder-in and can perform a few steps c
canter half pass.

He must allow me to control the cante
in terms of collection, straightness an
spring in all areas of the school.

PROGRESSION OF EXERCISES

1 I often start by doing counter canter on
large circle, and just as I approach the centr
line I increase the spring and activity an
give a small nudge with my inside leg, insid
to the bend of the horse (on the concav
side). This is sometimes reinforced with
quick touch of the schooling whip, 4 or 5 cr
(1 ½ - 2 inches) further back than the norma
leg position and no further. As a roug
guide, I deliver this signal just as the leadin
foreleg comes forward. When teaching,
often have to repeat the signal for the nex
stride as well.

I have a rule that I never *make* a horse dc
a change but only *ask* him, or coerce/coa:
him, to make one. It is, of course, possible t
swing the horse off balance, with a stron
twist of the rider's upper body and stron
leg and rein aids, thus making him execut
a change. However, this method does nc
reflect a confident understanding on th
horse's part and it also encourages rough
crooked changes from the very star
Therefore, it is a method which I do nc
favour at all.

As to the actual aids, as I have alread
mentioned, one has to vary the strength
sharpness and placing according to th
horse's reaction and this is something or
which your trainer must guide you. The
coordination of the timing of the half halt, or

Improve canter by sharp transitions to and
from collected to medium canter to improve
athleticism and increase height of moment of
suspension.

Crooked changes

Either the horse swings forehand, hindquarters or jumps to the side of the intended line.

Often rider-induced; if so, ensure that
rider does not swing upper body, pull on
new inside rein, or use too much sideways
push in leg aid. Most inexperienced horses
will often lose balance and fall to one side of
the line. Keep horse straight on new outside
rein. With thoughtful riding, experience and
confidence, most horses usually become
straighter.

The better the canter, the easier it is for a
horse to learn and perform flying changes.
You can judge a good canter by the expressive moment of suspension. The canter is a

pace of three-time and, after the final beat,
when the leading foreleg is leaving the
ground, there follows the all-important
phase of suspension when all four legs are
off the ground. It is during this moment that
the horse performs the flying change.

It follows, therefore, that the longer this
phase lasts and the more spring the horse
generates in the hind legs, the easier the task
of changing all four legs. It is rather like
trying to perform a somersault on a trampo-
line; if your jumps lacks height you may only
make it part of the way around.

On the subject of what aids to use when
teaching a novice horse, one cannot be too
narrow-minded. Individual horses react differently. Some are more sensitive to the leg,
while others are more lazy and still others
react by challenging the authority of the leg
aids in a rather aggressive manner. As in any

the new outside rein, is critical. If that sounds rather technical, an easy way to remember is that you deliver the signals with the leg and rein on the same side. In other words, to change from left canter to right lead: nudge with the left leg and half halt with the left rein at the same time.

You will also find that your horse changes easier to one side than the other and therefore requires different timing and sharpness between left and right. Eventually, with practice and time, they even up.

2 I do not like to do changes in the corner of the arena for, if the horse turns sharply to negotiate the turn, he can often be late or short behind.

3 Try to change from counter to true canter in the middle of the long side and, later, the short side of the arena.

4 On the diagonal from the quarter marker, coming out of the second corner towards the centre line marker (A or C), ask for one change quite early on this line and then, if the canter is under control, ask for a second change after five or six strides. It is not necessary to count the intervening strides, and the advantage of this line is that if the horse does not respond to the second change, one can simply turn into true canter when reaching the centre line marker and repeat from the other direction.

5 On the long diagonal, let's say KXM, ask for one change as you approach the quarter line, centre line and three-quarter line. This is the start of tempo, or sequence, changes but still do not be tempted to determine the number of strides beforehand. Instead, concentrate on the control, straightness of the line, and the correctness of the changes. If I feel the horse becoming tense and anticipating the last change, I often miss this out and make him stay in counter canter and then return on the following diagonal to repeat the move. This ensures obedience and calmness.

6 Slowly you will have become aware of the approximate number of strides you have been taking between changes and it is therefore a natural process to attempt changes perhaps every four and then three strides.

In teaching riders I have found, over the years, that they often find three-time changes easier to coordinate than fours. I am not really sure why this is, except that, rather like a line of jumps at related distances, the greater the space in between, the more likely they are to lose balance, quality and control. Inexperienced riders will often not wait for the fourth stride and therefore lose the timing of the aids.

7 Progress on to two-time changes, which do not usually present too much of a problem. Vary the place you practise them in the school, using the long sides as well as the diagonal. Keep returning to single changes to improve the straightness and quality of the technique. Use the serpentine and centre lines for variation.

8 One-time changes. I usually start these by asking for 'pair' as I turn across the school on the EB line, or on the short side. One has to have the second leg and rein aid in readiness almost before the horse has made the first change until he catches on to the exercises. As his understanding and reaction speed change, so must your timing also change accordingly.

9 After practising a pair of one-time changes in all the different places in the school, add another change to make three changes every stride. I am very careful not to perfect the pair of one-time changes as the horse can often think that is all there is to the exercise. In fact, we need to make him realize that he must go on continuing to expect the changes until he is told to stop.

This sounds rather idealistic, but you will appreciate that the speed of the exercise does not allow for a slow reaction on the horse's part. I always feel it is like a singer and pianist, who must both hit the note at the same time; neither can wait for the other, they must both be committed to the rhythm of the exercise.

Once the horse is happily doing three changes every three strides he will often offer more and, suddenly, the fifteen consecutive changes required at Grand Prix do not seem so very far away.

ABOVE
In spite of a slight twist in the rider, the horse performs a lovely expressive change.

LEFT
After the horse's right front leg has touched down, he will spring into the air and change from this right canter to the left. Although slightly exaggerated, this picture shows the delivery of a clear leg aid and the necessary straightness of the rider in flying changes. Notice also how he keeps the horse straight on the new outside rein, in this case the right rein.

CHAPTER
TWELVE
Pirouettes

Pirouettes demand maximum co-ordination from both horse and rider. They require quick observation and instant reaction in order to prevent loss of balance, activity and gait sequence.

Their purpose is to encourage and demonstrate greater weight-carrying on the hind legs; in other words, collection.

They are an important mark earner in competitions where the marks allocated are often doubled.

We shall begin our study of pirouettes with the ones performed in walk.

pecific faults other than those affecting the basic way of going.

Pivoting on the inside hind leg

ue to the size of the pirouette being too nall for the degree of collection, or to lack activity in the collected walk.

orrection: make the circular track of the nd leg slightly bigger and improve the sic collected walk, especially on the tivity and use of the joints of the hind leg.

Walk Pirouette – Priority Points

What it is

The walk pirouette is a movement whereby the horse's forehand moves around the hindquarters. In a perfect pirouette, the inside hind leg will be picked up and down more or less on the same spot. In training, walk pirouettes are introduced as quarter pirouettes through a 90-degree turn. In competitions, however, pirouettes through a 180-degree turn are required. They are introduced in competitions at approximately medium level.

Aim/Look for

Correct way of going (page 29).

Maintenance of the four-beat walk sequence.

Size of circle of the hind legs. Ideally, this should be with the inside ind leg being picked up and down more or less on the spot.

The fluency of the turning of the forehand.

The maintenance of the correct bend in the direction of the movement.

EFT and RIGHT
anter pirouettes require great collection and eight-carrying on the hindquarters. Notice the itting of the horse on the left. However, on the ght, the horse has almost over-reacted and brought is hind legs too far underneath his body. With nstant correction, this exceptional rider was able to ebalance him in the next stride.

The hind legs swing outwards away from the turn

Caused by lack of control of hindquarters.

Correction: use travers down the long side and then on a small circle to regain control of the hind legs. Ride a bigger pirouette with the hindquarters slightly in.

The forehand swinging round

Caused by lack of control of the forehand.

Correction: increase the size of the training pirouette and half halt every other step, sometimes include a full half halt.

Circle line of the hind legs too big

Probably due to insufficient activity in the collected walk.

Correction: improve collected walk. Practise tighter turns on the outside track to identify how large the circular track of the hind leg is, and then reduce.

Quarters-in during departure into pirouette

The horse is not controlled straight before the pirouette.

Correction: practise riding a small angle of shoulder-fore for the last few strides of the collected walk and then depart into your pirouette. Ensure that the horse is ridden absolutely straight on exit.

PROGRESSION OF EXERCISES

When the horse can do a small angle of shoulder-fore and travers, and is capable of a slight degree of collection:

1 From a medium walk, develop slightly more collected steps. Ride travers on the long side and then on a small circle, starting on 10 metres and reducing to 6 metres. Only keep the haunches in for 3 or 4 strides at a time and then go straight on the circle line.

2 While riding travers through alternate corners of a large square, turn your shoulders to encourage the horse's forelegs to take sweeping wider steps: you are now doing quarter pirouettes.

3 Across the school on the EB line, ride half pirouettes, ensuring that the horse is on the straight line before and after.

Once the horse is established in walk

horse to swing out, thus turning on the centre), to be able to turn his shoulders and forehand similar to entering the first step of shoulder-in, and to regulate the speed and size of the turning.

Never lose sight of the purpose of the movement, that it is to test and improve the carrying ability of the hindquarters and the control and influence of the rider. Thus, every stride must appear balanced and deliberate.

pirouettes and is developing sufficient collection in the canter, we are ready to consider introducing the canter pirouette work.

Canter Pirouette

To do good pirouettes you need two essential ingredients, firstly, the ability to collect and shorten the canter and, secondly, control.

The shortness of the canter refers to covering less ground in each stride and not merely shortening the neck, which is absolutely wrong. Not only do we need shorter strides but, almost more importantly, the horse must transfer and carry more weight on to the hindquarters. This is the fundamental test of the pirouette.

When I talk about control, I mean that you should have the ability at any one instant to move the hindquarters slightly in (to prevent the natural tendency of the

ABOVE
A correct canter sequence and controlled, yet fluent, turning of the forehand. However, for perfection, there could have been slightly more lowering of the hindquarters.

Common Faults

Specific faults other than those affecting basic way of going.

Hindquarters swing out

Caused by rider crookedness or too much inside rein. Also caused by horse's stiffness or lack of understanding/obedience to the rider's outside leg. Practise quarters-in or circles of varying sizes.

Hind legs jumping together

Improve quality and ease of the collected canter before repeating the exercise on larger circle.

Hind leg circle too big

Achieve greater shortness and collection of canter. Ensure good preparation in last two strides. Analyze which 'quarter' of pirouette is too big and half halt just before this point.

Forehand hurrying around

Caused by mental tension or loss of balance and control. Make bigger pirouette, either whole or certain 'quarters', to keep horse forward from inside leg.

Laboured, losing canter jump

Make bigger, and encourage more fluent turning of forehand by turning rider's shoulders into direction of movement.

Croup high, low in front

Canter incorrectly collected. Not taking weight on hind legs. Practise on circle, then straight, varying degree of collection and assessing correctness.

WHEN HORSE READY TO START

Horse must understand walk pirouettes. When the collection and shortness of canter is increasing enough to canter an 8-metre circle.

When horse established in canter shoulder-in, travers and half pass.

PROGRESSION EXERCISES

1 On a large circle, shorten canter until you feel the horse is almost cantering on the spot. Only keep for two strides. Then try on straight line. Count normal strides between two arena markers, then increase shortness to fit extra strides in. Later, try exercise on diagonal and eventually centre line.

2 Canter a 10-metre circle, ask for travers and hold for about three strides then return straight on circle. Repeat on a 6-metre circle. You are now doing some strides of a large

pirouette These are called working pirouettes. They are less demanding than tight, competition-size pirouettes and allow you to establish confidence, balance and fluency of the canter sequence.

3 Ask for a quarter pirouette during one of the corners on large square. Not on every corner, perhaps every third one. Try to encourage tighter pirouettes i.e. the right-angle is completed with the hind legs more or less on the original line in about two or three canter strides.

4 On 20-metre circle, as you go towards centre line, increase collection and ask for a working half pirouette. You can then continue on the original circle in counter canter and repeat the exercise; or if this is too much to think about, leave the circle and continue in true canter.

5 Next, try the working half pirouette on the diagonal. (See diagram page 50).

6 Progress to full working pirouettes on large circles and then diagonal lines. Analyze which quarter of the pirouette the horse attempts to enlarge or tighten and vary the exercise in contrast.

7 Reduce the size of the pirouettes down to competition size but always return to working pirouettes to improve technique and eradicate faults.

8 Place the pirouettes on the centre line.

As the horse becomes more familiar with the exercise, try to ride the last two strides on the approach, before the pirouette, in a small angle of shoulder-in. This will prevent crookedness on the approach and also encourage collection in the preparation.

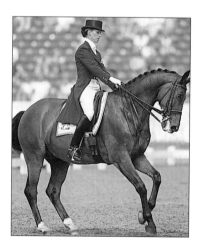
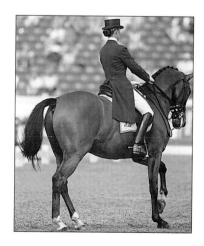

RIGHT
Some wonderful moments in Anky van Grunsven's pirouette to the left.

CHAPTER
THIRTEEN
Piaffe

The piaffe is one of the most demanding and exacting exercises at Grand Prix level. It should be the result of progressive training, aimed at transferring much of the weight of the forehand on to the hind legs.

It is performed in a trot rhythm and as the horse transfers the weight, lowering his croup towards a sitting position, he appears to trot almost on the spot.

BOVE and BELOW
me trainers start to teach the piaffe 'in-hand', see
ELOW. However, it is a progressive system which
quires great expertise. Note the lowering of the
rse's hindquarters and the energetic diagonal
ovement of the horse's legs. Later, this system
n be extended to include the rider, as ABOVE.

EFT
n active, balanced piaffe.

Piaffe – Priority Points

What it is

When the horse trots, almost on the spot. It
is introduced to tests at Intermediare II
level where horses are permitted to travel 1
metre forward in 7/8 steps.

Aim/Look for

Correct way of going (page 29).

Diagonal beat.

Lowering of the hindquarters towards a
sitting posture.

The correct placing, never backwards,
but creeping only centimetres forward
each step.

Regular rhythm.

Active, lively impulsion with horse
springing from step to step.

Even height and placing of hind feet.
Good height and equally flexed front legs.

Common Faults

Lazy, resistant

Poor preparation. Lack of understanding or confidence. Incorrect basic way of going. Make horse more sensitive in basic way of going. Progress steadily, asking for only a couple of steps at a time.

Hind legs more active and higher than front legs

Incorrect balance. Reduce activity and encourage more forward. Examine correctness of collected trot and encourage to sit and take more weight on the hind legs.

One, or both hind legs stepping back

Caused by loss of balance and drawing back from leg. Use legs more forward and encourage the horse to creep gradually forward on more even steps.

Narrowing base. Stepping too close or too wide

Incorrect balance and technique in training. Ask for less activity and allow forward. Some transitions to passage may help achieve a greater freedom of foreleg action.

WHEN READY TO START

When collection and all lateral work and single flying changes established. Always teach the piaffe before the passage.

BUILD UP/INTRODUCTION

Two main methods:
• By working 'in-hand' without a rider.
• Developing 'only two or three steps' under saddle.

Working in-hand

There are many variations of this type of work. For example, some trainers use long reins, others teach on the short rein.

This is a specialized area and should only be attempted under expert practical guidance.

Priority Points

Aim for correct 'sitting' posture and diagonal beats.

Always keep horse slightly forward in training.

CHAPTER
FOURTEEN
The Passage

ABOVE and RIGHT
Virtu and Emile Faurie say it all when it comes to passage. Note the self-carriage, height of the front legs and elastic activity of the hind legs. The rhythm is like clockwork and he is really passaging at both ends! RIGHT, a slight loss of balance has caused the horse to drop his poll and lose some self-carriage.

This is the proudest and most elevated 'dance' at Grand Prix standard. It is a perennial favourite with riders and spectators alike. However, it is also extremely demanding in terms of the horse's muscle power, concentration and balance.

Common Faults

Specific faults other than those affecting the basic way of going.

Irregular rhythm
Caused by incorrect way of going, incorrect technique or lack of engagement. Keep horse responsive and in front of rider's legs. Ensure good, correct impulsion and engagement in collected trot.

Hind legs losing active diagonal beat, almost walking
Caused by stiffness in back, lack of activity and swing. Achieve good, active, collected trot, then ask for only a few steps of passage and return to trot. Improve trot and repeat.

Swinging legs, not straight
Caused by crooked rider, aids too disturbing or tight, restricted top line muscles. Return to previous stages, especially forwards piaffe.

Lack of height/expression
Caused by lack of engagement and activity or lack of understanding. If former, achieve better, genuinely collected trot before re-trying. If latter, use piaffe as basis and gradually encourage forward in a more 'closed' active posture. Start when piaffe established.

INTRODUCTION AND PROGRESSION BUILD UP

1 From the piaffe, on the straight, gradually encourage forward whilst still keeping engaged and 'closed'.

2 Repeat and maintain for longer periods.

3 From trot, ask for only one/two steps of piaffe, then into passage.

4 Eventually try trot – passage – trot. The trot should give more impulsion and swing.

5 Repeat exercise on large circle line. Accustom horse to turning in passage. Start with wide, large turns and then reduce.

The Transitions
In the Grand Prix test, many marks are allocated to the transitions between the piaffe and passage.

They demonstrate confidence, obedience, suppleness and strength.

They need to be ridden with great tact and sensitivity in order that the two-time rhythm of both the piaffe and passage is not lost. You will often see the occasional walk or canter stride accidentally inserted when a horse is unable to sustain the movement.

Apart from the tremendous strength required in the horse's hindquarters, this is one of the greatest tests of harmony between horse and rider.

CHAPTER
FIFTEEN
Test Riding and Tactics

Test riding, or competition skill, is really only an extension and refinement of one's training technique. However, there are certainly some people who are better than others at presenting and highlighting the strong qualities of their dressage horse whilst camouflaging the weak areas. To be a good competitor you must learn how to perform in public and how to rise to the challenge of the sport.

By the time you come to the day of the competition you must accept one fact. It is too late to teach you or your horse anything new. If you have not got the extended trot or the flying changes by now, then you are not likely to perform them when you go into the ring. It all comes down to the work you do in training.

The basis of this test riding work is accuracy and preparation. The more we are able to ride into the corners, the more use we can make of the dressage arena. This gives us more space and more time to prepare our horse.

So, correctly ridden corners are the basis of accurate riding. As I mentioned earlier in this book, our training session does not begin until we ride into the corners and it therefore follows that neither does our test riding. It needs to be practised and both horse and rider need to be skilful enough and physically supple and balanced enough to do this.

First know your test

When I ask my pupils before a competition, 'Do you know your test?', they are very quick to reply and recite it from start to finish. But that is not really what I mean. That is only the course of the test as laid down on the paper.

What you must do is find out how your horse is going to react to each one of those movements and thus how you will prepare him, both in distance and before the marker, and how strongly or softly you will deliver

the preparation aid. You will know the horse's ability and level of competence through each individual movement and will draw up your tactics accordingly. For instance, it might be better to go for a cautious medium trot if the horse isn't yet fully established in this part of his training and try to make up the marks in another part of the test.

As to learning the actual course of the test, which in international competitions must be ridden from memory, there are many different ways of doing this. Perhaps the most often used is to walk through the test on your feet. Many top riders still use

this method and then incorporate mental imagery while they negotiate the test. This gives them a chance to mentally rehearse the reactions they hope for and anticipate.

Another method that I often use when I am learning a new test or a free style test, is to use the time that I spend at the beginning of each training session walking on a long rein; actually to walk through the course of the test. During this time I am telling myself whether I would be in canter, or trot, or riding flying changes. Several repetitions each day ensure that I walk the horse for long enough at the beginning of the session and learn the test at the same time.

When studying a new test on paper, I try to imagine blocks of movement in my head. It might be two half passes sandwiched by an extended trot or the flying changes with the canter pirouettes in between. My final test, to ensure that I really know where I am going, is to imagine the mental block situation. This occurs when we have been concentrating on the way of going of the horse, have failed to prepare for the next movement and have a complete blank as to what to do next. It happens to the best of us and it is therefore necessary to address it rather than avoid confronting the situation. I overcome this problem by ensuring that if I were to stick a pin into any part of the test sheet I would immediately be able to state the next movements. Sometimes, I even make riders tell me the test backwards and then forwards again, which is another way of ensuring absolute knowledge of the course.

Minimizing the effects of mistakes

Before we make any entries into any competitions, we have our own assessment competition at home. Here, we try to reproduce the same conditions, within reason, that we might expect to find at the show. For instance, we always work in the indoor school and then walk down to the outdoor school, which allows us the chance to practise maintaining the horse's concentration between these two places: many riders 'lose' their horses between the warming up and competition rings.

We then run through the test from start to finish, no matter what goes wrong. It is all too easy to put in the occasional circle or to do that centre line turn once again. But in the competition we have only one chance. We must learn how to ride and present the horse in such a way that we can capitalize on and maximize his strong points. We must learn how to react when things are going wrong, how to get out of a sticky patch, perhaps when the horse breaks from counter canter.

With novice riders I even teach and practise what they should do should they forget the test. Each error, of course, is penalized. Even the top riders have penalties deducted for an error of course at some point or another.

Should you hear the judge's bell during your test, do not over-react and instantly stop what you are doing, for you may actually only have imagined it, or it could have been a bell from another arena. However, if you are sure it was from your judge or that you have made a wrong course, go to the President of the Jury who is the judge sitting at C, who will tell you what you should have done. If you are still unsure, you can cleverly check by confirming the following movement as well! Ask the judge from what point they would like you to pick up the test again as this will be dependent on where the last mark finished.

Do not be flustered and disheartened. If you are able to reproduce some good quality work, then the penalties for a first error of course may have very little bearing on your final placing. It is only if you allow this error of course to upset your riding that things will go rapidly downhill from this point on.

During our rehearsal at home we often video the test in order that we can later analyze the good and weak movements. We develop a policy for long-term improvement and short-term presentation, which are not always one and the same thing. I believe that in dressage competitions we are fundamentally competing against our own riding and training skills, and what we are presenting to the judge and the public is the quality of our homework.

However, preparation and quick reaction are the hallmarks of a competitive rider. This requires thinking through possible undesirable reactions as well as imagining the good ones. What will you do if the horse starts to make a good piaffe two or three metres earlier than the marker? How will you react if the horse slips in a flying change towards the end of an extended canter? How long should you go on insisting that

the horse stands still in the halt instead of letting him fidget around?

There are no clear answers to these questions and much will depend on the importance of the competition. For the bulk of the competitions that we do, our job is to school for the long-term and the big occasions. Often, we are in qualifying competitions which just get us through. This gives us a chance to implement schooling policies whilst riding our test. The point is that too much covering up or compromising in the arena at the early stages of a horse's career will give him the wrong idea and wrong attitude later on, during the big time.

Dressage riders have one big advantage over show jumpers and eventers. We know the test we are going to ride and the sort of surface that we shall be expected to ride on before we leave home. Therefore, if our practice competitions at home produce a satisfactory result, there is no reason why we should not be able to reproduce the same standard if we just keep riding and preparing – and even correcting in the ring – as we have done at home.

Sometimes, the atmosphere at a show can even help the horse by giving him that extra bit of impulsion and sparkle. If I can achieve 65 per cent of the mark when practising at home, then I will be lucky to get 62 per cent in a competition situation. You must always allow for a fallback and therefore train to a higher standard at home than you would expect at the show.

Preparing for the competition

When I get to the show, I like to go and sit and study the arena before I warm up my horse. I like to see if there are any deep, wet patches and ask some of the riders how the arena is riding. I also study how I shall be riding in and around the arena and how much room there is to turn when making the entry. I note whether the judge is using a bell, a whistle or a horn and how clear and loud this is.

I like to sit at the A end of the arena and imagine myself riding through the test. I visualize the preparation and the half halts before each movement, the differing strengths of the extensions at various points throughout the test, and so on. Each rider has his own particular method of approach to this mental rehearsal. I do not necessarily

watch what my competitors are doing, because whether they have a good or difficult ride is of no consequence to me. The only thing that matters is that I focus on my horse, myself, and our partnership, in the hope of producing our personal best standard.

Dressage is not like other sports where as competitors we have to outwit or outmanoeuvre rivals. In a jump off, a show jumper can make a quicker or tighter turn which puts pressure on the riders coming after. In dressage, in order to get more marks, it is a question of doing the movements better and more accurately.

The quality of the movements can only be influenced by the training, but now the accuracy and the harmony between myself and my horse can only be achieved by us both being in a correct frame of mind and doing a successful warm up.

I will have planned the sequence of my warm up, the essential movements that I must include and the non-essential. I will decide at what point we will remove the boots or bandages or invite the steward to check the bridle and how I will ride between the collecting ring and the main arena. By then, I will have decided how I will ride around the arena before the judge's bell. Is there spooky flag flying in the wind that I should ride shoulder-in to encourage the horse to look in the opposite direction and ride it with a bit more power as I pass that area, or should I keep making plenty of transitions between the paces to ensure that harmony is maintained? In international competitions, we are not allowed to ride with the whip. When should I get rid of this?

From an accuracy point of view it always helps if you are able to sit in the judge's box or judge's car at lower level competitions and observe what is apparent to the judge and what is not. If this is not possible, you may be able to offer to write and act as secretary to the judge. Although one is not able to see as much, it is still a very valuable exercise and something I would recommend to all aspiring competition riders.

The world's greatest actors and actresses all confess to having attacks of stage fright before they go on. In fact, they say it is necessary in order to get their adrenalin flowing and to stimulate their very best performance.

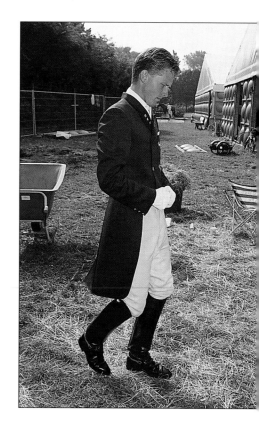

Therefore, try not be worried by an attack of nerves; instead, use them and channel them in the best possible direction. Do not allow nerves to tighten up your muscles, as tension in the arms, back or legs undoubtedly makes for confused signals to the horse. Take several deep breaths before you go in and make sure that, as you ride down the centre line, you are breathing deeply and regularly.

After each movement, when you are riding on the short side, it is important to produce an elegant, supple and yet active way of going. This gives you a chance to repair any factors which have adversely affected the previous movement and allows the judge to take in the general picture.

One must not have allowed the secondary stresses of the competition atmosphere to put you in the wrong frame of mind. For instance, forget a bad journey, traffic jams, an over-officious steward or even an enthusiastic but tactless remark from one of your support team who, after all, may themselves have no first-hand experience of competing.

After your test and when your horse is correctly cared for, you must think through the good and the bad, and understand where and why any problems arose. Were there weaknesses in the training or was there a breakdown in communication between horse and rider or a poor signal from yourself which contributed to the mistake? It is important that your appraisal of your performance is matched against that which you could reasonably expect to achieve, knowing your horse's current training level. Obviously, if your trainer is at the show, then you should discuss the test with him.

Only after you have made these observations should you go to the score board and see how that particular judge compared your performance with others. We all like to win and it is very good for our confidence and for that of our support team. However, we must be scrupulously honest and decide if we were the best of a bad bunch or whether, in fact, the lower placing in a strong class is more than acceptable.

We must take our performances over a number of tests and see the common denominators in terms of strong and weak points arising. The judges' percentage marks are perhaps of more help to us in our long-term development than our immediate placings.

CHAPTER
SIXTEEN

... and Finally, It All Hangs on the Warm up

After all the dedicated training, rehearsal, planning and preparation is done, we add the last piece to the jigsaw, the all-important factor of a successful warm up.

The object of warming up, or riding-in as it is often called, is to bring the horse to peak performance during the test.

Each horse, and rider, has an individual method and period of time best suited, and this will vary and change during the phases of training and individual circumstances affecting the competition, such as locality, atmosphere and so on.

There are four phases to the warming up period. It is important at shows that the rider does not adopt any new method or technique that has not usually been included in their training sessions. In fact, it is essential that the rider does not do anything different or introduce any new exercise. There are occasions when one is competing a horse a a level that is not yet established and it is al too tempting in the riding-in to practise a movement at which the horse is not ye fully proficient.

What one has to remember is that i the horse hasn't really been able to grasp that particular exercise in training, he is not going to start learning it in the

0 minutes prior to the test. Over-practice of that particular movement could well result in a loss of confidence and harmony in the ensuing tests. Much thought must be given in the run-up to a competition as to the exercises included or left out during the actual warming up at the show.

So, much thought and a careful eye on the clock is required to secure a good warm up for a test. Before getting on your horse, check with the chief steward whether your arena is running to time. It is no good bringing your horse to the boil to discover that the judges are running 15 minutes late!

First phase of warming up

This is the phase that cannot be shortened or hurried. It will include the gradual and progressive stretching and suppling of the horse's muscles and many of the exercises that one does on an everyday basis. However, there are certain factors which may lengthen or shorten this phase and cause a different reaction from that to which we are accustomed.

The length of the journey and the effect of travelling must be taken into account. This is particularly relevant with older horses, which can often stiffen up during a journey, or with young, inexperienced horses which may have been slightly worried by the journey.

The exciting atmosphere of the showground can often cause horses to be rather fresh and excitable. Thought must be given as to how you should best cope with this. If the horse is given too much work to settle him down, then he may not have enough energy to perform well during the test. With both these conditions, it might be better to walk the horse round either in-hand, to let him stretch his legs and perhaps pick up a little bit of grass, or just to exercise the horse around until he calms down and loosens his muscles.

Another factor which can influence the length of time required to warm up is whether the horse is preparing for the second test, in which case the period will obviously be shorter as the horse will have a limited amount of energy in reserve.

Second phase of warming up

The aim of this phase is to secure the engagement of the horse's hind legs and to channel the impulsion through a supple back, neck and jaw. It is really a précis of the early part of your normal training session and aims to secure a good way of going, and in the shortest possible time, in order that the horse's impulsion and concentration level is preserved.

From your daily training sessions you will have learned which particular exercises are most effective with your individual horse. You will know which lateral movements supple him up the best, and employ many transitions, both from one gait to another and within each gait, to help him to engage his hindquarters.

The horse will finish this phase when he is supple, engaged, and active enough to respond instantly to the rider's sensitive aids for the half halt. He is thus tuned in to the rider, both mentally and physically.

The suppleness and looseness achieved in phase one will allow you to straighten the horse, centre his balance and have him in a 'state of readiness'.

Third phase of warming up

It is essential that the rider knows the test. By this, I don't merely mean the course of the test as laid down on the dressage sheet, but the particular movements that an individual horse finds easy, relatively difficult and very difficult.

For instance, it might be coming back from an extended canter or trot followed by the turn up the centre line. It could be shoulder-in on the centre line followed by 10-metre circles right and left. Each horse has his strengths and weaknesses and these particular areas vary throughout a horse's training. I personally think it is essential to practise the difficult and, in fact, the easy parts of each test plenty of times at home. Lots of people are worried about practising the whole test from start to finish in case the horse should start to anticipate.

If this is a worry, then you can practise particular movements from the test but in a different order or even in different places in the school. You can then identify the difficult component or difficult part of the movement and work on that individually before returning to the task of stringing a few movements together.

Now, to get back to the warming up and the parts of the test that you know will benefit from repetition and practise in the warm up, and those that you know will not. For example, with some particular horses practising too many extended trots can get them too lit up, while with others it might be quite a good thing.

Some horses would benefit from repetition of flying changes and some that, per-

haps, are not very established, need to do just a few good ones and leave it at that. For some, it might be sensible only to practise the halt and rein back on the centre line once or twice and then to finish off by just halting on the centre line to make sure that the horse doesn't step backwards of his own accord.

These are just some examples of the effect of repeating certain exercises that we need to know before we leave for the show. So often, you see riders, new to advanced level testing, running through it almost from start to finish in the warm up arena. This is not necessary and will only serve to tire a horse or make him peak while he is still in the warm up arena.

I always remember the saying 'Never leave your test in the collecting ring'. You have to decide whether you want your horse to look impressive in the collecting ring or impressive in the actual competition arena in front of the judges. At a big show, where you can have a large crowd watching the warming up show, do remember that it is not their opinion that is important. Do not show off to them, but bring your horse steadily to his best in order to impress the judges and not the crowds.

It is important that throughout the warming up, the rider and trainer keep their eyes on that clock. The horse will need sufficient breaks in between each phase in order to have a breather and mentally relax. It is no good going into the ring with a horse out of breath and pouring with sweat.

Fourth phase of warming up

Having practised your pre-selected test manoeuvres in the third phase, you will often find it necessary to go back to the basic way of going on the single track work for a few minutes before you go into the ring. For instance, it may be that the effect of practising the extended trot might put the horse on the forehand or that practising the trot half pass has lost some impulsion or engagement of the hind legs.

It will therefore be beneficial to remind him of the all-important basics: balance, impulsion, rhythm, straightness, suppleness and calmness. Have the horse well in front of the leg, over the back and into the rein contact.

Do not overlook the logistics

Make allowance in your time schedule for plenty of rest periods, for time to remove the boots or bandages or to give the horse a quick wash or scrape down. At big competitions and every international event, the steward will have to check your tack to see if you have got the correct bit and other permitted saddlery, and this can take a few minutes. Equally, make a note of how long it takes to walk the horse on the aids from the warm up arena to the stadium. Sometimes this can take longer than you think.

It is always an advantage to arrive at your arena with as much time to spare before the judge's bell, as you are allowed by the steward without, of course, disrupting the previous rider's final test movement. This will allow you extra seconds for re-tuning whilst being in the midst of the competition atmosphere.

If you are at a big competition, the horse may have been a little unsettled by the applause for the previous rider, the loud speaker, perhaps a television camera

ABOVE and RIGHT
Happy and relieved it's all over, or is it? The journey to perfection never ends, so it's back home and, after a balanced appraisal, it's down to further training before you're ready for another show.

winging around to face him. Remain calm and put your 'professional' training into operation. You have practised for this and every other eventuality. You and your horse will soon be working in perfect harmony.

Do you hear the judge's bell? You look to the judges' stand and – yes – the Chief Judge is standing waiting to return your salute. The audience settles, now there is silence. Your adrenalin is flowing. You feel your heart thumping. This is good. You rise to the occasion. You put your nerves to positive use. You remain focused on your horse, totally focused. Seconds pass. You are oblivious of the audience, of the judges, of the environment.

Good luck, you're now 'in the groove'.
See you at the scoreboard!

'Practice does not make perfect – only perfect practice makes perfect.'

79

INDEX